BRISTOL AT PLAY

BRISTOL AT PLAY

Five Centuries of Live Entertainment

KATHLEEN BARKER

MOONRAKER PRESS

© 1976 K. M. D. Barker
First published in 1976 by Moonraker Press
26 St Margarets Street, Bradford-on-Avon, Wiltshire
SBN 239.00160.5

Text set in 10/11 pt Monotype Plantin, printed by letterpress,
and bound in Great Britain at The Pitman Press, Bath

Contents

Acknowledgements

The idea for this book originated in a talk given at Redland College, Bristol, in January 1972, when I was asked to choose a subject which would make the students 'more aware of Bristol's long and interesting theatrical history'. I hope that in its present form this rather longer but still necessarily incomplete study will stimulate interest in the multi-faceted world of live entertainment in Bristol from the earliest recorded 'mummers' to the most 'experimental' street theatre the roots of whose appeal are so similar.

If I have been successful in doing this it will be thanks no little to Miss P. K. Stembridge of Redland College and Miss Sybil Rosenfeld of the Society for Theatre Research, who have read and commented most helpfully on the draft.

Among the many other people to whom I am indebted for information and help I should also particularly like to thank the following:
Miss Mary Williams, Bristol City Archivist, who took such personal interest in finding information about the Wine Street theatre site and the City Fairs; Mrs C. Brewer, Archivist of the Society of Merchant Venturers, who made a special search for references to the Jacob's Wells theatre and the George Inn; the staff of Bristol Reference Library for endless patience and resource in locating source material; Mr Francis Greenacre, Curator of Fine Art at the Bristol Art Gallery, for his help in finding and supplying illustrations; Mr T. Woodward, manager of the Bristol Hippodrome, for permission to reproduce the photograph of the interior; Professor Glynne Wickham for permission to use his transcription of the BM manuscript dealing with Henry VII's visit to Bristol; Miss O. E. B. Youngs for checking and correcting my transcription of Nicholas Woolf's will; Mr David Illingworth, not only for information on the Avon Touring Company and other recent developments, but for introducing me to the redoubtable Joe Baker; Mr W. Solway of Shirehampton, Mr Frank Wilson of Horfield and Mr W. Hitchings ('The Great Valdo') of Bishopston, who wrote and talked to me about the old days.

An earlier version of Chapter Three was given at a Manchester University Drama Department Symposium in 1973 and is to appear as a paper in *Western Popular Theatre*, ed. D. Mayer and K. Richards, Eyre Methuen.

KATHLEEN BARKER

ONE

Pageants and Players

1461–1729

'Bristol is not celebrated for patronising Public Entertainments,' complained Charles Dibdin the younger in 1799. 'There is no disguising the fact that Bristol is not a playgoing place,' lamented the *Bristol Standard* in 1840. Even in 1914 the *Bristol Times & Mirror* critic remarked: 'The Bristol public are a peculiar lot to cater for.' In view of this, perhaps it is appropriate that almost the first we hear of live entertainment in Bristol is when in 1479 the Mayor and Sheriff

chargen and commanden on the Kyng our souverain lordis behalf that no maner of personne of what degree or condicion that they be of at no time this Christmas goo a mommyng with close visageds [i.e. masked]. (*Ricart's Calendar*, 18 Ed. V)

Perhaps these gentlemen had forgotten that 18 years previously they had greeted the newly-crowned Edward IV with a fine 'mommyng': a mercifully brief address by his ancestor William the Conqueror at Temple Gate; and at Temple Cross a mime of St George slaying the dragon. And only seven years after the ban, Henry VII was welcomed with a most elaborate emblematic pageant including

an Olifaunte, with a Castell on his bakk, curiously wrought. The Resurrection of our Lorde in the highest Tower of the same, with certeyne Imagerye smytying Bellis, and al went by Veights merveolously wele done.

The entertainment also included a speech from the legendary founder of Bristol, King Brennus, lamenting the decay of local trade, and asking for the King's help in remedying the causes of the city's poverty, in which he was so successful that the historian of Henry's progress commented: 'The Meyre of the Towne towlde me they harde [had] not this hundred Yeres of noo King so good a Comfort.' (BM Ms Cot. Jul. B XII)

There is, regretfully, no evidence for religious Guild plays in Bristol such as York, Coventry or East Anglia could boast. Certainly the Mayor's Calendar records that towards the end of the fifteenth century, on St Katherine's Eve, the Mayor and Corporation returned to their homes after a feast at the Weavers' Hall 'redy to receyue at theire dores Seynt Kateryns players, makyng them to drynk at their dores, and rewardyng theym for their plays'; but this suggests a very secular money-collecting *quête* on the lines of the St George plays (and modern carol-singing). Certainly, too, the records of the Bakers' Guild in the sixteenth century mention payments to minstrels, and to bearers of the 'pageant', but again these seem to refer to civic processions and celebrations, and there are apparently no references to dramatic usage.

What existed before any of these records, and until long after permanent professional theatres were established in Bristol, was entertainment at the great Fairs, notably that of St James in the Horsefair, which dated back to 1374, and rather later that of St Paul, or Temple Fair, granted by Edward VI to be held every January from 1550 onwards. St James's Fair, in July, became one of the most important trade fairs in the country, the Admiralty even sending ships of war to protect vessels carrying goods thither in 1630. Jugglers, minstrels, puppeteers, strolling players and entertainers of all kinds flocked to the Fairs to reap their own harvest from the incomers. The degree to which fair entertainments became established is attested by the fact that when in 1636 the Corporation negotiated about the rights of Temple Fair with the parishioners and Churchwardens, the 12 parishioners executing their part of the indenture included no fewer than three describing themselves as 'showmen', John Young, Richard Nelson and Maurice Reynolds.

Corporation records also bear witness to more official visits, from 1532 onwards, of a stream of private theatrical companies attached, sometimes rather nominally, to the households of members of the royal family or nobility in order to escape being categorised as vagabonds. By custom, on arrival they gave their first performance before the Lord Mayor and Aldermen in the Guildhall in Broad Street, for which they were paid in earlier years 6s 8d (33p) or 10s (50p), but as the century wore on these amounts doubled, and by 1600 they had risen to £1.50 or even £2.00.

Although it is very unlikely that Shakespeare himself ever came to Bristol, the two greatest tragedians of his day, Edward Alleyn and Richard Burbage, certainly did. The Alleyn papers at Dulwich contain a letter from him written in Bristol on 1 August 1593 to the 'good mouse' his wife, dashed off just before he went to play in *Harry of Cornwall*.

There were not only companies of men and boys visiting the city, but tumblers, drummers, waits and bearkeepers; 6s 8d was paid in August 1569 'to my Lord of Norfolks bereward for batinge his beares . . . in the marshes' (i.e. what is now Queen Square). Of the popularity of at least some of the companies there is good evidence. In 1576 6d (2½p) had to be paid 'for two ryngs of jren to be set vpon the howces of thonside of the Yeldhall dore to rere the dore from the grownd and for mending the cramp of jren wch shuthyth the bar wch cramp was stretched with the press of people at the play of my Lord Chambleyn's surts [servants] in the Yeldhall before Mr. Mayer and thaldermen'. On other occasions the Corporation had to repair the Guidhall doors, and forms borrowed from St George's Chapel which were broken in the scrimmage.

In 1574 Queen Elizabeth visited Bristol on one of her progresses, and the city put on an elaborate, expensive and excruciatingly tedious pageant for her. Two castles were erected, one representing Feeble Policy and commanded by Dissension, which was eventually overthrown by the defenders of Peace. The text of this three-day spectacle was subsequently printed by one Thomas Churchyarde, Gentleman, under the delightful title of *The Firste Part of Churchyard's Chippes*, and in it he complains that some of the speeches included in the published version 'could not be spoken, by means of a scholemaister, who envied that any stranger should set forth these shows'. The Queen can only be said to have benefited from this professional jealousy.

Something more tangible came from the state visit of James I's consort, Queen Anne of Denmark, in 1613, when she was entertained by 'Orations, Gifts, Triumphs, Water-combats and other Showes', some of which she had seen already elsewhere. At her request James issued a special Patent unique in the provinces[1] to John Daniel, brother of Samuel Daniel the poet, permitting him to raise a company called the Children of Her Majesty's Royal Chamber of Bristol.

Information on the troupe is scanty: they can only twice be traced playing in Bristol itself, in 1622 and 1623, and seldom elsewhere. In June 1618 the Mayor of Exeter refused them leave to play because the Patent stated 'Youths and Children' but the company was composed almost entirely of men, with only five youths; in his *English Dramatic Companies 1558-1642*, J. Tucker Murray suggests that the original company had amalgamated temporarily with an adult troupe, the Queen's Company, but split up again soon afterwards.

There is, however, evidence of a private playhouse in Bristol in the early years of the seventeenth century, originating in a Wine Street house abutting on the chancel wall of Christ Church at the top of Broad Street. Nicholas Woolf, a cutler, leased this house, and an adjoining strip of land 16 feet deep, for 41 years from 1598, covenanting to rebuild the whole within four years. The resultant building is referred to in Woolf's will of 1614 repeatedly as his 'play house in wynstreete', and he left sums out of the rents issuing therefrom to various charities, including Queen Elizabeth's Hospital School, with the proviso that such rents 'to be paid out of my said Playe house shall continew due and payable soe longe only as the same house shall continew a playe house at (*sic*) that such players as doe resorte to the said Cittie or inhabite within the same Doe usually playe there and maye be permitted and suffered quietly to playe there and noe longer.' A nineteenth-century transcript of Queen Elizabeth's Hospital records which have not survived shows that their legacy ceased after 1619; in April 1620 the lease of the Wine Street premises was transferred to Anthonie Bassett, a tailor. Local authority enthusiasm for the players was on the wane all over the country in the seventeenth century (by 1630 Bristol Corporation was paying actors 'to send them out of the citty'), and the presence of an

---

[1] A similar Patent was granted to York, but no use seems to have been made of it.

established provincial playhouse at this period, however restricted in size it must have been, is almost unique in the annals of the Elizabethan and Jacobean theatre.

The last trace of visiting players in the Bristol Treasurer's accounts is in 1635, and there was unlikely to have been much if any live professional entertainment during the Commonwealth, even after the fighting was done; but almost immediately after the Restoration the Fairs were back in full swing. The size of the pleasure fair at St James's may be surmised by the fact that Sir Henry Herbert, Master of the Revels, thought it worth while to send one of his messengers there in 1663 to extort licence fees from providers of 'musick, Cockfightings, maskings, prizes, Stage players, tumblers, vaulters, dancers on the ropes, such as act, sett forth, shew of present any play, shew, motion [puppet show], feats of activity, or sights whatsoever'. John Latimer in his *Annals of Bristol in the Seventeenth Century* has a number of references, not all of which can be verified, to the licensing (or prohibition) of entertainments at the Fairs, and one to 'the place where the play is in Christmas Street'. It is clear that the Corporation were continually being torn between moral disapproval of the strolling entertainers and material hankering after the rents for the standings. Eventually St James's Parish compounded with the Corporation for the Fair rights in return for an annual payment.

From 1704 to 1706 Bristol was visited by a more regular theatrical company, based on Bath, and using the name of The Duke of Grafton's Servants, its leader being John Power. The only contemporary evidence is contained in an anti-theatre pamphlet of 1706 by the Vicar of Temple, the Rev. Arthur Bedford, called *The Evil and Danger of Stage-Plays*, including transcripts of various complaints to the Grand Jury of Bristol about Power's company. From these it appears that Power acted by permission of the Corporation within the liberties of the city during 1704; returned to a site 'near that *City*' in July and August 1705 with elaborate promises that only the most moral plays would be staged by him; and in the summer of 1706 performed in a 'newly-erected *Playhouse*', once more within the liberties. A strong but late eighteenth-century tradition places the first theatre in Tucker (now Bath) Street, which is quite feasible, as this was in Bedford's parish and near the entertainment area of Temple Fair; and the third in St Augustine's Back, on the site of the present Radiant House, where certainly there was an established playhouse in the 1720s. The site of the second theatre is unknown, but one of the 'Long Rooms' at the Hotwells is a possibility. Once in 1704 and twice in 1706 aggrieved citizens 'presented' Power to the authorities; there is no evidence that any action was taken, and none as to whether his company returned in subsequent years.

Indeed, of Bristol's theatrical history during the next two decades next to nothing is known. This was the period when, according to his biographers, the young Charles Macklin took engagements as a strolling player in Bristol, Bath and South Wales—a 'Bristol Company of Comedians' is found in Monmouth in September 1724. With the survival of a few of Bristol's early newspapers from 1726 onwards, however, it is possible to say with some certainty that a theatre on St Augustine's Back was in regular use by 1726, when we find Charles Williams, a supporting actor from Drury Lane, starring in a summer company.

In December that year Fisher's puppets—'Figures 5 foot high [which] move Heads, Eyes, Mouth, and all parts of their bodies to the Life' (a description which needs to be accepted with some reserve)— performed *The Earl of Essex* and *Henry II*, first at Lloyd's Warehouse on St James's Back and later at the Rose and Crown in Tucker Street: 'The Part of King Henry II by a little Boy, and all the rest of the Parts to the best Advantage.'

In 1728 the St Augustine's Back theatre was occupied by a pantomime troupe of acrobats including Madame Violante, who 'discovered' Peg Woffington when she was a Dublin slum child; they were later joined by an acting company led by Thomas Lewis. They had, however, rivals in the Bath Theatre Company, who had brought to the Long Room in Hotwells, and later to their Great Booth in Bridewell Lane, a reproduction of the triumph of the London season, Gay's *Beggar's Opera*. Gay himself had instructed the players, and when the London season was over, the Somerset actor John Hippisley, who had made his first great success as Peachum, joined the company. By 24 August they had played the opera 43 times in Bristol, and then went off to Wells to repeat their success, leaving Lewis's Company, who 'have made the town ring of their fine Performances'.

But fame can have its disadvantages: in September both playhouses were 'presented' as 'publick Nuisances and Nurseries of Idleness and Vice'. The Bath Company having strategically left the city, the Mayor issued a warrant on 6 November to apprehend Lewis. In the resultant scuffle the Chief Constable himself was assaulted by an indignant member of the audience, which can have done nothing to improve the official attitude towards the stage.

Almost certainly this episode influenced John Hippisley in deciding that if he was to invest his money in a theatre of his own in the Bristol area, it would have to be outside the city boundaries—and the obvious alternative was to take advantage of the fashionables who came every summer to drink the waters at the Hotwells, a mile-and-a-half along the bank of the Avon, at the foot of the steep cliffs leading up to Clifton. So, shrewdly, Hippisley sited his theatre on the Gloucestershire side of Woodwell Lane (now Jacobs Wells Road), accessible from both the city and the spa. The *London Weekly Journal* of 28 June 1729 reported:

Bristol June 21. We are now building a very spacious Theatre at Lime Kilns lying convenient for Coaches as well as for the Rope Walk leading to the Hot-Well.

On 23 June Hippisley's company opened their season with Congreve's *Love for Love* in their new theatre near Jacob's Well, and the drama had again 'a local habitation and a name.'

TWO

Theatre becomes established

1729–1800

Of the earliest years of the Jacob's Wells Theatre almost nothing is known, as few newspapers and no playbills have survived. In 1736 the playhouse was reported 'completely finished', though what had previously been lacking, it is impossible to say. For its physical appearance we have to rely on the description given in Richard Jenkins' *Memoirs of the Bristol Stage* (1826), which indicates that it was a typical small provincial theatre with boxes set about an oblong pit and extending on to the stage; above the boxes was the gallery, and over the stage doors were smaller boxes known as 'pigeon holes' which gained a rather unsavoury reputation.

For the years 1741–48 the Account Books survive in the Bristol Reference Library, and provide not only information on the company and repertoire but detail of the finances. On the early nights of the season a deduction was made every evening to cover rent, music, lighting (by candles), ancillary services and any special properties or costumes required; after which the balance (if any) was shared equally among the players on a 'commonwealth' basis. Mrs Hannah Pritchard, the great tragedienne of her day, stipulated for a clear £50 for the season, but this was exceptional. Even Charles Macklin, returning to Bristol after his London triumph as Shylock, was 'on shares'.

Towards the end of the season each player had a 'Benefit' performance, whose proceeds he kept after paying the expenses of the night and five-shilling shares to his colleagues. To encourage Bristolians who were chary of returning across Brandon Hill after dark, link-boys might be promised, and a moonlight night was worthy of special mention. 'Madame CYNTHIA will appear in her utmost splendour,' advertised Richard Winstone on a later occasion, and found himself in dire trouble with an audience agog to see this gorgeous foreigner.[1]

Accounting was scrupulous, down to 'a shilling lost on ye Stage' and the forfeiture of a share as a penalty for absence from rehearsal. Receipts

---

[1] But at least he had looked in the Almanac and found out moonshine, as the Zoological Gardens proprietors were reminded when in 1870 they advertised a Grand Moonlight Promenade Echo Concert on the night of a lunar eclipse.

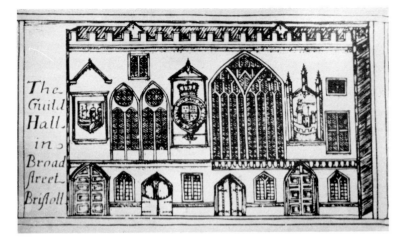

The old Guildhall, Broad Street, where Elizabethan touring companies played before the Mayor and Aldermen. Engraving from James Millerd's 1673 map of Bristol.

Part of Millerd's map showing site of Guildhall (L) and of Nicholas Woolf's playhouse near Christ Church (N).

The Fourteen Stars, Counterslip, off Temple Street, used by showmen such as John Seward during Temple Fair. Engraving in Richard Smith Collection, Bristol Central Library.

The Assembly Rooms, Princes Street, opened in 1756 and used for every kind of entertainment in its 160-year span. A hotel now occupies the site; Assembly Rooms Lane, leading to the harbour, still exists. Watercolour by T. L. S. Rowbotham, by permission of Bristol Art Gallery.

King Street in 1825, showing the Theatre Royal and Coopers' Hall on
left; extreme right is the Old Duke public house, later a tavern music
hall. Watercolour by T. L. S. Rowbotham, reproduced by permission of
Bristol Art Gallery.

Principal Entertainment Sites up to 1800

1 St James's Fair
2 Temple Church,
  focal point of Temple Fair
3 Guildhall
4 Woolf's playhouse

5 Tucker Street Theatre
  (conjectural)
6 St Augustine's Back Theatre,
  later Assembly Rooms
7 Great Booth in Bridewell Lane
8 Jacob's Wells Theatre

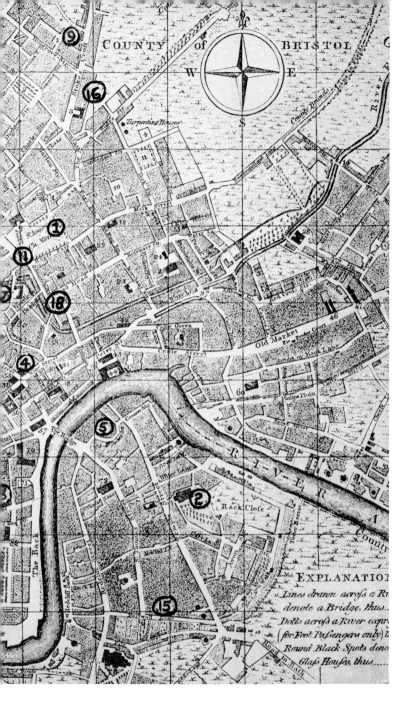

St James's Fair

Cider House Passage showing (centre) the Taylor's Hall and
(right) the Raglan Tavern Concert Hall. Engraving from Skelton's
Antiquities of Bristol.

Bristol Mercury engraving of Charles Samuel Bartlett, strolling
player and murderer, whose crime contributed to the suppression
of St James's Fair.

Harry
Clifton.
-from
an old
chalk
litho

Little brown
jug

Jolly
Nash.

P.S. Just a memory of
Old Court
Minstrels,
our one
and
only

Horace

Sketches by F. G. Lewin of famous music hall personalities of
the late nineteenth century: Harry Clifton, Jolly John Nash, and
Horace Livermore as a 'blackface' Court Minstrel in George II
costume. Published in *Bristol Times & Mirror*, 12 May 1923.

show a steady rise over the period from an average of about £10 a night in 1741 to nearly £20 in 1747. In May of 1747 the theatre was reported 'lately enlarged and beautifyed', with a new set of stock scenes—the ground landlords, the Society of Merchant Venturers, had insisted on at least £50 being spent on improvements when granting Hippisley a reversionary lease. Hippisley was left sufficiently short of money to have to borrow £240 on mortgage, despite raising the nightly allowance for 'rent' from three guineas to four. Unfortunately he died on 12 February 1748, and though the following season went through as planned, there was a marked falling-off in receipts except when some specially appealing attraction offered.

The next decade seems to have been rather bleak, and the theatre was abandoned for at least one season. Mary Hooke, widow of a former J.P., coffee-house owner and printer, who had 'supported herself and Family for several years past, by Means of Printing the Play-Bills for the late Theatre in Jacob's Wells' reported in August 1757 'That the Theatre now being shut up, she is thereby depriv'd of her sole Dependence and Subsistence.' (*Felix Farley's Bristol Journal*, 13.8.1757)

Despite the passing of the 1737 Act of Parliament which made illegal all theatrical performances for hire, gain or reward other than those in theatres possessing a Royal Patent or special licence, there is no evidence that the Jacob's Wells company was ever prosecuted; not only its site but its fashionable clientèle from the Hotwells were in its favour. The danger, however, was always present, and other performers playing in or near the city confined themselves usually to mime, recitations or 'concerts'. A tumbling troupe headed by Mons. and Mme Dominique gave pantomimes 'with all the Machines and Decorations proper to the Entertainment' at a theatre in Stokes Croft in February and March 1744, with occasional plays. When they departed, the theatre was taken over by a strolling company of actors led by a Mr Marshall, who even obtained Masonic support for the Benefit of one of their number, Stepney, on 4 May, when the Masons arrived in full regalia, the stage being 'built proper for their Reception'.

This building, like Jacob's Wells, was just over the Gloucestershire boundary at the time, being sited about where Jamaica Street now joins Stokes Croft, but that does not seem to have saved the actors from legal action, judging by the fact that the Jacob's Wells company that summer gave an extra performance on 3 July 'for the Benefit of Mr. *Marshall*, in Confinement'.

In November the following year the Dominiques returned with their 'celebrated Company from Sadler's-Wells', but this time the difficulties they met stemmed from international events. The panic arising from Charles Edward Stuart's landing in Scotland, allegedly with the backing of France, set off the usual excess of chauvinism. By February 1746 Dominique had to advertise:

Mr. *Dominique*, (being sensible that he has suffered greatly in the opinion of the Town this Winter, by being supposed to be the Master of a French Company, at a time when an unnatural Rebellion is supported by France against his Majesty's Crown and Dignity) thinks he should be wanting to himself (*sic*) if he did not endeavour to remove those false Impressions, by assuring the Publick that not one Person of his whole Company is of that Nation; that he himself is of *Bern* in *Swisserland*, Madam *Garman* of *Amsterdam* in *Holland*, Mr. *Jonno* of *Milan* in *Italy*, and that all the rest are *Natives* of Great Britain. (*Bristol Oracle*, 1.2.1746)

But the damage was done, and in mid-March Dominique gave up, never to return to Bristol.

Outside the avowed theatres, entertainment was centred on the fairs, where waxworks and mechanical models bid for patronage against such attractions as the African Hermaphrodite (with anatomical explanation in Latin), the stiff-rope exercises of Mrs Reverant, and Powell the Fire Eater. Two well-known figures from the London fairs, the comedian Richard Yeates and the dancer Adams, brought a company to the St James's Fair in 1749 with a continuous programme of farces and pantomimes lasting from ten in the morning to nine at night. From 1750 the Merchant Taylors' Hall in Broad Street was also a recognised home for itinerant entertainers who wanted something better than the Great Room of some inn, and to this Hall Adams returned in December of that year, giving what he advertised as 'A CONCERT of VOCAL and INSTRUMENTAL MUSICK' with a medley of entertainments including a pantomime and a display of the Manual Exercise by the notorious Hannah Snell, a transvestite who had served many years in the Army undiscovered under the name of James Grey. Adams remained there till February 1751, but May of that year found him presenting a full theatrical programme of plays, dances and pantomimes at the New Inn 'without Lawford's Gate'—i.e. just outside the City Liberties. He advertised for patronage, 'Mr. ADAMS's Circumstances not admitting him to pay his Respects to his Friends'—was he under threat of legal proceedings?

Another frequent visitor to the Bristol Fairs for very many years was the showman and puppeteer James Seward; in his later years he held the post of City Trumpeter in Bristol and died in prosperous circumstances unusual for an erstwhile stroller. His nephew, son of Tom Maddox the rope dancer, who ended his days 'keeping a Vauxhall in Moscow', told C. J. Harford in 1786: 'Many a time I have acted Punch, and played on the Salt box in the gallery at the corner of Silver Street, and Seward is my uncle who brought me up from child,' after Maddox senior had been drowned.

The Great Room at the corner of Silver Street and the Horsefair was indeed generally known as Seward's Room.

Testimony to the close watch kept by the authorities on theatricals is provided by Mrs Charlotte Charke, daughter of the great theatre manager, Colley Cibber. She was briefly employed by the *Bristol Intelligencer* about 1752, and to eke out her miserable wages arranged with a strolling company, of which her daughter and son-in-law were members, and which was currently acting at Wells, to give a Benefit performance for her at the Raven Inn, High Street: 'All was to be done under the Rose,' she explains in her *Narrative of the Life of Mrs. Charlotte Charke*, 'on account of the Magistrates, who have not suffered any Plays to be acted in the City for many Years.' The company does seem to have escaped the law, but the Benefit, alas, turned out what Mrs Charke wittily rechristened a 'Malefit'.

After being abandoned by players following the building of Jacob's Wells, the theatre on St Augustine's Back was adapted some time before 1742 as an Assembly Room, a contributor to the *Oracle* of 25 September 1742 describing the change derisively:

> THE House which was built, as the Founder once swore,
> To furnish an Al—r—n's Son with a Whore;
> And since has been used, as 'tis very well known,
> By the Player, the Fidler, the Dancer, Buffoon;
> Will now, more commodious than ever before,
> At once entertain and receive them all four.

Initially used mainly for balls and concerts, it reappeared as a home of theatrical entertainment after the building of the New Assembly Rooms in Prince's Street, which, bearing the legend *Curas cithara tollit* ('Music relieves the burdens of care'), opened in January 1756 with a performance of *Messiah*, and for the next 20 years attracted many of the most fashionable concerts.

Instead, to St Augustine's Back came Tom Maddox, the great slack-wire performer; the Jacob's Wells actor turned schoolmaster, Rosco, in a course of oratory; and a succession of tumbling and acrobatic troupes of self-styled Prussians and Italians. Although the Merchant Taylors' Hall in Broad Street was more convenient for St James's Fair, the St Augustine's theatre was saved from becoming a backwater by the mid-century shift of fashion towards Queen Square, and since it was also on the main road to the Hotwells, it continued to be used intermittently for concerts and entertainments till the early 1770s, when it was converted into a Chapel for Lady Huntingdon's Connection.

The city did not, of course, have the monopoly of non-dramatic entertainments. The Jacob's Wells Theatre drew as much on the inflated summer population of the Hotwells as on resident Bristolians, and the Long Rooms there were in regular requisition for entertainers and musicians; John Seward too had a room known by his name at the Hotwells as well as at St James's Fair.

Besides these, there were recurrent attempts, all of them disastrous, to build up a pleasure garden on the lines of London's Vauxhall. The site of one such, at the back of the Long Room, was advertised to be sold in 1741; ten years later the opening of New Vauxhall was delayed 'by Reason of a Master Carpenter's deceiving [Charles, the proprietor] in the Execution of his work;' further hindered by slanderous reports of bad faith and of the employment of French musicians; and finally washed out by rain. Charles survived the rivalry of Perrott's Wells with its Virgin's Well and show grotto at the top of Nine Tree Hill the following year, but 1753 found him complaining once more that his enemies were luring away his employees, and buying up tickets to resell

9

at cheap rates 'to the meaner Sort of People'; and at the end of this season he gave up. Charles Claggett attempted a revival of Vauxhall in 1757, but in 1761, according to Latimer, the ground was sold for building.

The increasing prosperity and expansion of Bristol between the late 1750s and the outbreak of the war with America were reflected in the world of entertainment. New genres made their appearance both in and out of Fair times; the touring solo entertainer edged round the letter of the law by presenting, with Mayoral permission, a miscellany of music and sketches under a suitably fanciful title, blending sentiment with mildly satirical commentary on contemporary manners, or selecting songs and recitations to illustrate some compelling theme. In January 1763 Tate Wilkinson, later one of the most successful, and certainly one of the most colourful, provincial theatre-managers of the century, brought his 'Dish of Tea' (modelled on Samuel Foote's device to elude the law at the Little Theatre in the Haymarket) to the Assembly Rooms, and was sufficiently encouraged to return in November the following year. Thomas Sheridan, father of the dramatist, gave Readings at the Merchant Taylors' Hall in August 1763, offering free tickets to those who subscribed to his new English Dictionary. The Coopers' Hall, built in 1744 to the financial ruin of the Guild, and used variously as commercial school, dancing academy and saleroom, was pressed into service from 1756 onwards for courses on Oratory, Lectures on Heads (by George Alexander Stevens and his imitators) and on Hearts (by a Miss Adcock), and for the occasional tumbling troupe and medley company.

Equestrian performances also began, humbly enough, in this period, in the shape of riding exhibitions on the Downs. Thither came T. Johnson in July 1758 and Thomas Price in June 1763.

> UPRIGHT he stands, and swift as rapid Tides,
> With Ease at once—upon three Horses rides:
> Now on a single Steed he scours the Plain,
> Flying dismounts—without the Dread of Pain,
> And now as quick as Lightning mounts again . . .
> (*Felix Farley's Bristol Journal*, 11.6.1763)

In October 1772 Philip Astley himself brought the first equestrian troupe to Bristol and displayed in a roped-off enclosure on the Downs over 40 feats of horsemanship, ending with a comic burlesque.

Participating in the new prosperity, the Jacob's Wells Theatre reopened in the summer of 1758 under John Palmer of Drury Lane and Matthew Clarke of Covent Garden, and it was not long before Palmer was advertising at his Benefit that

In order to prevent the Entrances from being crowded, so that the Performances may be conducted with Ease . . . an Amphitheatre will be erected after the Manner practis'd at the Theatres-Royal in London. (*Felix Farley's Bristol Journal*, 21.7.1759)

This involved erecting tiers of seats at the back and sides of the stage, thus considerably cramping the performers, though it had the merit of confining the audience to specific areas and preventing them from wandering backstage. It became increasingly clear that a new and larger theatre, taking advantage of the shift of fashion within Bristol, would be needed, and, insulated against the perils of the law by the high civic position of many of those concerned, a group of 40 citizens met on 17 September 1764 and formally agreed 'to Erect and Build a Theatre or Playhouse in the City of Bristol', on a plot behind some houses in King Street next to the Coopers' Hall, within a stone's throw of Queen Square and the Assembly Rooms.

Two events in particular probably helped to precipitate this action. The most important one was the acquisition in the summer of 1764 of the latest star of the London stage, 29-year-old William Powell, who had stepped into Garrick's parts when the latter went on a Continental tour, and made a *succès fou*, which he repeated at Jacob's Wells. The poet Chatterton, the blue-stocking Hannah More, and a host of versifiers attested the rapidity with which he became the idol of the theatregoing public and the tears he evoked. For his first Benefit he converted the unpopular 'pigeon holes' into Boxes at the top price of 3s, 'the better to accommodate a greater Number of Ladies,' who were invited to send their servants to keep places for them three hours before the curtain rose. When it was over, Powell inserted a card of thanks for the support he had obtained, 'and further to express my Concern that the Accommodations of the Theatre at Jacob's Well are so very much unequal to so polite an audience.' (*Felix Farley's Bristol Journal*, 18.8.1764)

The second event which may have influenced theatre supporters was less pleasant. The company generously gave a special performance on 3 August 1764 'for the Benefit of a Distress'd Family'. Immediately they were beset by requests on behalf of another deserving case, but there were no free days left. An immediate donation and a date the following season were offered, but failed to satisfy the petitioners, who 'threatened, that unless their Demand was complied with, they would put a Stop to that Night's Performance; and accordingly, as soon as the Curtain was drawn up, the Players were saluted with a loud concert of Whistles, Catcalls, Groans, Hisses, and other agreeable Noises of the like Kind.' Finding reasoned remonstrance useless, Powell and his fellows, with the help of sympathisers in the audience, launched a physical counter-attack, 'and those unfortunate Politicians, together with their Mercenaries, were turned out of the Gallery, amidst the universal Shouts of the Audience.' (*Bath Chronicle*, 6.9.1764)[1]

The project for a new theatre in King Street went forward without check, though not uniquely it took twice the time and more than twice

---

[1] There is no evidence that the Jacob's Wells Theatre was ever used after the summer of 1765; though Hippisley's daughter, Mrs Jane Green, retained the lease till 1786, the building fell into increasing disrepair, and Society of Merchant Venturers' records prove that it was finally demolished some time between 1803 and 1826, a group of tenements known as Cottage Place being erected on the site.

the money originally estimated. When it was eventually opened on 31 May 1766 its impact was immediate.

When the whole was illuminated, there then appeared one of the finest Scenes Imagination can conceive; the rich Paintings, together with the Brilliancy of the Ladies, formed so complete a View, that Malice herself, had she been there, must (for that Night at least) have put on a Smile of Approbation. (*Sarah Farley's Bristol Journal*, 21.6.1766)

The first-night visitor who penned that rapturous description saw, of course, a very different theatre from the one we know to-day. The frontage then consisted of a cluster of seventeenth-century houses, through and behind which passages were constructed to the pit and boxes. Were his ghost to return, he would find almost as drastic a change within. The forestage, originally coming past the first boxes, has now gone, altering the whole character of productions; and the present proscenium arch is a hotchpotch of alterations with unusable relics of proscenium doors where once were principal stage entrances topped with boxes. Behind the arch everything has now been destroyed, including what had been a unique survival of the back-stage recess used for scenic effects of distance. The original building lacked the present Gallery; its ceiling was flat and in the attic space over it the scenery and properties were painted, a state of affairs which continued until 1837, when the Fire Insurance Company belatedly jibbed at the risk involved in the use of oil stoves up there. The floor of the pit was flat and its seating consisted of bare benches.

There would still be some features which a Georgian ghost would recognise; the colour scheme of green, gold and brick-red (though applied now, quite illogically, to Victorian decorations); the horseshoe curve of the balconies, and the gilded square pilasters of the stage boxes contrasting with the fine reeded pillars elsewhere. Both the last two features were novelties in 1766, and they created quite a sensation among theatre connoisseurs.

The new Bristol Theatre initially evaded the letter of the law by advertising 'A Concert of Music interspersed with Specimens of Rhetorick', but even this thin disguise was dropped when the growing respectability of the acted drama was marked by the proprietors of the neighbouring Bath theatre in Orchard Street securing a Royal Patent at the beginning of 1768.

Until his death in the summer of 1769, William Powell continued to be the leading manager of the summer companies which used the theatre. As at Jacob's Wells, the great majority of the players still came from the London theatres, and included many of their leading actors and actresses —Charles Holland, James Dodd, Ned Shuter, Thomas King, James Quick, Mrs Jane Barry, Elizabeth Younge and many more—together with a varying number from the Bath Theatre Royal, among them John Henderson, the finest Shylock since Macklin. Though generally prosperous, its conduct was by no means without occasional scandal; one manager, Samuel Reddish, notorious for bringing a different 'wife' with him each season, and who was also subject to intermittent fits of lunacy, precipitated outright rebellion among his company and finally walked out on them in mid-season. James Dodd, despite Charles Lamb's sympathetic portrait of him, was another trouble-maker as manager; a notorious womaniser, conceited and unreliable of temper, his weaknesses inadvertently led to the legalising of the New Theatre in King Street as the Theatre Royal.

In the late autumn of 1772 a well-organised strolling company under two ex-London actors, Laurence Kennedy and John Booth, set up in Coopers' Hall under the dubious legal protection of giving Concerts of Music 'with divers Specimens of ELOCUTION'. They put on a well-varied programme, and with no alternative entertainments in Bristol save a civil war between two rival promoters of subscription concerts (the only effect of which was that both lost money), the patronage was good; the theatre proprietors scented dangerous rivalry, and were worried.

Dodd came blustering down to Bristol declaring he would horsewhip these upstarts out of town, which of course brought more support for Kennedy and Booth and exposed his own vulnerability: he could hardly initiate action against the interlopers without reminding authority that his own performances had been illegal. Consequently the Proprietors hastily made application to Parliament for a Patent while organising an 'information' against Kennedy and Booth.

They failed to get the requisite Act passed on this occasion, and even a swingeing fine of £200 did not prevent the completion of the Coopers' Hall season. But when the undaunted company, after a summer at Richmond, returned in 1773, the law pounced again and this time the leading actors were imprisoned and the season was abandoned. A second attempt in 1778 to obtain a Patent was successful, and citizens looked forward to all-the-year-round performances with pleasure or horror, according to outlook. 'How that may affect the morals of our sons, daughters, apprentices and servants, when they can conceal themselves by the darkness of the night, is but too apparent,' gloomily prophesied the author of a circular letter headed *An Alarm*!

After a rather uninspired winter season by the Exeter Company, the managers of the Bath Theatre Royal, who had long been regarded as the obvious lessees, moved in during the spring of 1779, and for the next 38 years ran the two theatres as a tightly-knit and most successful circuit, to the permanent exclusion of London summer visitors. It was a shrewd business move, for the popular playgoing seasons in each city dovetailed most usefully, while the cities were close enough, and the transport organised by the managers efficient enough, to make it possible every week to play one night in one city (it was always Saturday in Bath, Monday in Bristol) and three in the other.

The Bath Company was proverbially the chief recruiting ground for the London theatres, and its standards were probably the highest in the provinces. The leading lady at the time of the union with Bristol was Sarah Siddons, whose tragic powers were as emotive as Powell's had been, but just as able and popular in their own line were, for example,

Charles Murray, who played the 'heavies' for eleven years; the Edwins, father and son, both notable low comedians; Charles Knight, who struck off the manners of the dandy and the spark as to the manner born; and his wife Peggy, who by contrast specialised in country lasses (typecasting was nearly as rigid as in Victorian melodrama).

These and many more made most successful London careers in due course; but perhaps the best loved figure of them all was the manager and leading actor, William Wyatt Dimond, who spent virtually the whole of his professional life in Bath and Bristol. His qualities both as actor and manager were not less sterling for being unspectacular, and at his best—as, say, Hamlet or The Stranger in Kotzebue's gloomy drama—he was impressive and moving. Above all he inspired a rare degree of affection and respect not only in his audiences but his actors.

Though the communism of the sharing system had long given way in Bristol to carefully graded salaries, a successful Benefit was still vital to any actor's financial security, but so many things—excessive heat, an epidemic, a sailing match, an election—could spoil it. In the turbulent anti-French atmosphere of 1794, poor Knight was horrified to find scrawled on street walls 'Damn Knight—Knight is a vile Jacobin.' He seems to have convinced his audience to the contrary, fortunately, for his Benefit raised £139, one of the best results that season. Indeed, though notoriously Bristol was slow to respond to a new name (even Robert William Elliston only took £40, barely house charges, in his first season, though a leading actor), once established in the city's favour a performer could count on a generous bonus in this way.

The establishment of a regular theatre did not monopolise the audience for entertainment, however; rather it stimulated a demand for more, and more varied, provision. The encouraging climate even inspired the creation of a new Vauxhall Gardens, this time on the Somerset side of the Avon opposite the Hotwells, in the summer of 1776. This was managed by a Mr Williams, whose patrons journeyed by ferry or coach to enjoy music and fireworks out of doors (when the weather permitted) on evenings carefully chosen not to clash with performances at the Theatre Royal. The first season, however, ended on a thoroughly farcical note, with William Boyton, a temperamental musician from the theatre orchestras who seems to have had some share in management responsibilities, complaining that he could not illuminate the gardens on the night of his Benefit as 'Mr. WILLIAMS . . . removed the Lamps off the Premises'. To this Williams retorted that the lamps belonged to him, and that he had previously warned Boyton to settle his debts first,

Or did he expect Mr. *Williams*, after Mr. *Boyton's* contemptuous Behaviour during the Season, wou'd have come to him Cap in Hand, and made him an Offer of the Lamps, for never having paid or offer'd to pay a single Shilling for his Attendance these three Months past, not a *Penny* out of *Seventeen Pounds*, Mr. Williams advanc'd to pay Servants, &c. (*Felix Farley's Bristol Journal*, 10.8.1776)

The next season the Gardens were taken over by Kingsbury, leader of the Band, but within weeks his losses were such that he had to dismiss two of his London singers with part of their salaries unpaid, and the poor ladies, Mrs Beaumont and Mrs Maples, had no recourse but to organise themselves a Benefit Concert. In July Kingsbury gave up concerts and fireworks to concentrate on refreshments—'Beans in Perfection and Strawberries Ripe'—but it was too late. *Felix Farley* for 13 September advertised the sale of effects of 'Mr. WILLIAM KINGSBURY, a Bankrupt', including a four-stop organ, two guitars and some German flutes. With the gradual running down of the Hotwells, there ended for some 50 years the recurrent attempts to add a Pleasure Garden to the amenities of Bristol.

In other respects, however, the last 20 years of the eighteenth century provided a rich variety of shows and showmen. The pleasure section of the Fairs, especially of St James's Fair (which from 1770 onwards took place at the beginning of September, when the Theatre was closed),[1] became so considerable that by 1788 the moralists were petitioning that it should be shortened.

One feature of the fairs was always the supply of freaks: the Corsican Fairy, the Irish Giant, the Learned Pig, and the Spotted Indian Youth, whose owner indignantly denied the rumour that 'the white spots on the Indian Youth, are the work of art'. Menageries were generally popular, and could be put forward as educational as well; Cross blackmailed his visitors by advertising admission prices as 'Ladies and Gentlemen 1s. —Servants, &c. 6d.—But why should I mention this?—Generous and honourable Souls, scorning to deviate or demand price will always pay like themselves.' Towards the end of the century a feature was made of panoramas, sequences of painted scenes like primitive newsreels on canvas, usually picturing episodes of the war.

Besides these, both in and out of Fair times, there were regular visits from conjurors, notably Philip Breslaw and the romantically-named Highman Palatine; and troupes of tumblers and musicians who were able to find audiences in the Old Assembly Room, the Merchant Taylors' or Coopers' Hall for weeks at a time. In July 1766 Mrs Sarah Baker, later to become 'Governess-General and Sole Autocratrix of the Kentish drama', brought 'the usual diversions of Sadlers Wells' to the Old Assembly Room, delightfully burlesquing the elaborate advertisements of her rivals:

The Candles to be snuft in the French Taste, by a Gentleman for his own Diversion, being the first Time of his appearing in that Character . . . The Doors to be opened at Six o'Clock, and to begin exactly at Seven; and no Money to be returned that is fit to keep.

N.B. The what-we-call Theatre to be illuminated with Lights, and the Whole to conclude with being ended. (*Sarah Farley's Bristol Journal*, 5.7.1766)

They stayed all through July and most of August, and wound up with a 'dramatic Piece call'd A Wife well managed; or, a Cure for Cuckoldom'

---

[1] The date of Temple Fair was changed to the beginning of March by the same decree.

and a new pantomime, advertising 'Admittance to the Boxes gratis'—
a cheap enough offer, since there were none. By the 1770s there might
be four or five visits from such bands in a year.

Other entertainments of a theatrical nature were not lacking. Italian
Fantoccini (marionettes) took the Coopers' Hall in April 1781 to perform
Kane O'Hara's musical play *Midas*, and demonstrate a puppet Harlequin
who

will bring a Bottle of Wine in one Hand a Glass in the other, pour the
Wine from the Bottle into the Glass and drink it as natural as a living
Man to the Surprise of the Spectators. (*Sarah Farley's Bristol Journal*,
14.4.1781)

Performers from the Royal Circus produced musical pieces 'WITH a
grand Display of SCENERY and MACHINERY' at the Merchant Taylors'
Hall in November 1789, including *Liberty Triumphant*, 'a new piece,
grounded on authentic facts.' The following year Bates and Bristow,
from the Theatre Royal company, took advantage of the St James's Fair
to put on a topical entertainment called *A Touch at the Times*, 'the Whole
to conclude with the FREEDOM of FRANCE, or the TRIUMPH of LIBERTY'
with a grand mechanical procession. A few years later, when the
idealism of the Revolution had given place to the threat of Bonaparte,
either feature would probably have got the entertainers run out of town.

Many well-known names appear among those who sought the Mayor's
permission to give their lectures, monologues and recitals: George
Alexander Stevens, the London comedians Robert Baddeley and Lee
Lewes, Charles Dibdin the elder, and most frequently John Collins,
whose *Evening Brush to Rub Away the Rust of Care* became a feature of
many a season. Collins had started his career as an actor with the Bath
Company in 1759, and retained a special affection for the region; indeed
in 1792 he meditated taking up residence at the Great Grove House on
Redland Hill to establish a school for Young Gentlemen:

from the bustling Scenes of public life, [he] retreats to enhance the sweets
of retirement, with something worthy to employ his time, and with
impatient avidity to discharge a duty which he has long been conscious
he owes to Society. (*Bristol Mercury*, 3.7.1792)

He himself proposed teaching English and Belles Lettres; visiting
masters would be engaged for Languages and Mathematics. However,
like many another artist, he postponed and postponed his projected
retirement till another ten years had passed.

The last decade of the century saw the first semi-permanent establish-
ments in Bristol for what was to become a powerful rival of the theatres,
the full-scale equestrian troupe. After Astley in 1772 there was a long
gap, but in April 1788 the Royal Circus performers Ben Handy and
Thomas Franklin organised a group of their fellows and brought them
to the yard of the Angel Inn on the Borough Walls. 'The Place is genteelly
fitted up for the reception of Ladies and Gentlemen, and the whole of
the front seats is cover'd over, to prevent the company being incommoded
in case of rain.' (*Sarah Farley's Bristol Journal*, 26.4.1788.) They stayed

for a month, returned to the same site for the St James's Fair the following year, and removed to the back of the Full Moon in Stokes Croft in 1790, where they erected 'a very commodious Amphitheatre' in March. Here the troupe performed from mid-March to May, and from the end of August till mid-October, giving £16 profit to the Infirmary as a public *douceur*. Meanwhile the two had advertised for a subscription of a thousand guineas to build a more permanent Riding School, which they opened, rather surprisingly, in Limekiln Lane on the way to Jacob's Wells on 6 March 1792.

This by now somewhat out-of-the-way site did not prevent the success of the enterprise, even after a split between the partners only two months later (one of Handy's young apprentices taking the opportunity to abscond), for one or other continued to use the Amphitheatre for several months of every year. The attractions ranged from pony races to a mock fox-hunt: rather gruesomely an advertisement for Handy's Benefit in March 1794 explained

The Fox that is to be hunted on the above Night, is that which gave Mr. Coke (of Norfolk's) hounds such a long run the beginning of last season, and was taken alive. (*Felix Farley's Bristol Journal*, 15.3.1794)

Soon other circuses were coming in and near the Fair times, setting up temporary booths; with one such company in the summer of 1799 was Charles Dibdin the younger, later a manager of Sadler's Wells and deviser of pantomimes for Grimaldi. In his *Memoirs* Dibdin records how a wooden arena was knocked up at the foot of Union Street, and drew good houses; he himself was looking forward to a bumper Benefit, having puffed it well, when a few days beforehand an overflow house, dispersing in a rush, caused the gallery to collapse. 'Many were maimed, there were some fractured limbs, and one poor Woman so much bruised that she died in the Infirmary within a few days.' Of course this catastrophe destroyed public confidence, and poor Dibdin received only £2.37½ on his night, which did not even cover his advertising costs.

Such disaster was mercifully rare; indeed it was not to be long before the popularity of equestrian performances led to their transfer to the regular theatres. For it should always be remembered that, outside the so-called 'legitimate' drama, which was the prerogative of licensed or Patent theatres, there was a tremendous range of entertainment concerning which there were no preconceived assumptions in the public's mind about what belonged in a theatre and what belonged outside it. Spectators were quite likely to find acrobats, rope dancers, solo musicians or bird imitators on the stage of the Theatre Royal; the Little Devil's tumbling troupe were engaged three times between October 1783 and December 1784 and drew audiences from as far away as Exeter. Many of the fair booths went as far as the law would let them—and probably much further—in dramatic entertainments. Most concerts took place in the Assembly Rooms, but some were put on in the Theatre, where the management staged Oratorios in Lent for several years.

The gradual blurring of demarcation lines, which was to reach its apogee in the next half-century, may be partly accounted for by the change in appeal of the Theatre Royal once it had to draw its audience, not from an aristocratic elite taking the waters on a summer expedition, but all the year round from the rather less cultured middle-class Bristol mercantilists; even the gallery would now be filled, not with gentlemen's gentlemen, but with apprentices and shopworkers who had to be lured to scrape together the necessary shilling (no small sum, if you 'lived in' and your money wages were at most £5 a year), and later with soldiers and sailors seeking diversion from the Wars. By the 1790s it is clear that the audience had become appreciably less genteel and the repertoire was being modified accordingly; the 'Gods', then located in the central portion of what is now the Upper Circle, were beginning to make their noisy presence felt in no uncertain manner.

Nevertheless, if not quite so classical in its repertoire as once it had been, the Stock Company maintained high standards. The close links with the London theatres fostered by the transfer of so many actors and actresses were of benefit to the circuit in other ways also: in the chance to acquire, often within weeks of production, the newest London plays and afterpieces, or to borrow special costumes and properties, as was done for a performance of *King Henry VIII* in January 1780. The managers were ready to plough back profits, not only into rich decor, but in redecoration of the theatre and other material improvements.

They reaped their reward in enthusiastic audiences, aided by the popular pressure for escapist entertainment which wartime always brings. When their lease ran out in 1799 they were confident enough to accept a renewal for 18 years, and to promise not only better backstage facilities but the insertion of a separate gallery, which enlarged the capacity of the house by something like 300 people. In Bristol as elsewhere in the provinces, theatre seemed unassailably established.

THREE

The Circus comes to Town

1801–1853

It is clear from their willingness to invest money in enlarging the Theatre Royal, Bristol, and five years later in building a new and bigger Theatre Royal in Beaufort Square, Bath, that the Stock Company Managers felt themselves riding a wave of prosperity. Even the retirement from acting of William Wyatt Dimond appeared not to diminish the attraction of the company, which still boasted Robert William Elliston as leading man, comedians like Andrew Cherry and John Edwin junior, and such promising young actresses as Julia Grimani and Sarah Smith. Continual troop movements in and around Bristol (there was a big encampment on Durdham Down) contributed an important element to theatre audiences while the wars with France lasted.

But, at least in Bristol, there were soon signs that appearances might be deceptive. Dimond's continuation in management after leaving the stage meant that the theatres were now obviously being controlled from Bath, and the opening of the new Beaufort Square theatre seemed to many Bristolians a clear sign that managerial interests were increasingly being concentrated on the rival city. And if there is one thing guaranteed to damn an artistic enterprise in Bristol, it is allowing its citizens to feel that the management has its sights set elsewhere, and that Bristol is only of secondary importance in achieving its aims. Such a feeling began to build up after Dimond's retirement, aided by the traditional distrust in which each city held the other, and by the fact that for all his professional ability, Dimond's successor as Acting Manager, Charles Charlton, carried no real responsibility in the administration.

Traces of managerial insecurity can be seen as early as January 1802 in an obviously inspired comment on a London report that the boxers Belcher and Gamble had been engaged at the Bristol Theatre Royal for ten guineas a week:

We presume there is no necessity of contradicting so injurious a report to the inhabitants of the city; but only think it prudent to apprise strangers, and more particularly the Metropolis, in justice to the reputation of the Manager, that it is wholly unfounded, and has arisen, as we imagine, from the circumstance of Belcher and Gamble being at present engaged with a troupe of itinerant Equestrians, &c., who are exhibiting in this city.
(*Bonnor & Middleton's Bristol Journal*, 9.1.1802)

To whom this particular troupe belonged, we do not know, though equestrians did indeed frequently visit Bristol. After Handy and Franklin had faded from the scene, the Limekiln Lane circus site fell into disuse, and visiting troupes normally confined their visits to the Fairs. Since at this period the Theatre Royal opened only on Mondays at the time of Temple Fair and was closed during the St James's Fair, they provided little direct competition, and when the engagement did clash, the circuses, like other entertainers, avoided Monday performances.

Bannister was the most regular circus manager visiting in the first decade of the nineteenth century, and his performances generally continued the eighteenth-century traditions of trick riding, tight and slack rope exhibitions and other acrobatic feats. Occasionally there was something more: in January 1803 Saunders erected an Amphitheatre in Nelson Street, and in February his manager Davies from Sadler's Wells began to produce quite elaborate pantomimes such as *Harlequin Statue, or, The Fairies' Gift*, 'to conclude with a most superb Representation of a CORAL GROT; or, NEPTUNE'S PALACE; With Tritons,· Mermaids, Dolphins, &c.'; and later *The Witch of the Oaks, or, Harlequin Mariner*,

the whole of this magnificent and interesting Spectacle to conclude with CUPID'S PRESENT: And the Theatre, by means of new and singularly constructed Scenery and Machinery, arranged in different gradations apparently moving by Magic Power, forming the *Stage* into *a Representation of Cupid's Triumph*, May be considered as one of the first *Coup de Theatres* ever beheld. (*Bonnor & Middleton's Bristol Journal*, 19.3.1803)

Apart from the circuses, there were intermittent visits from individual entertainers, including the old favourite John Collins, whose wife's ill health, requiring 'the Hotwell water and the air of Clifton', brought him to Bristol in the Spring of 1806, when he was persuaded to give some further performances which included not only the well-loved 'Brush' but a phantasmagoric display. Collins' publicity was marked by an unusual honesty about priorities: 'The applause he receives is universal, but the substantial patronage transcends the applause.'

Phantasmagoria—early magic-lantern shows with stereoscopic ghost effects—were all the rage in the early years of the century. The Theatre Royal managers themselves seem to have been first off the mark with displays in February and October 1802; two years later there was a demonstration of apparatus made by a local optician, J. Springer of 2 Clare Street, of 'a grand PHANTASMEIDOS . . . where PHANTOMS will be seen flying in air.' In December the following year, Belzoni, 'the Patagonian Sampson' [*sic*], showed his Phantascopia at the Trout Tavern, Cherry Lane, off North Street, ending with 'His Grand HYDRAULIC Exhibition of FIRE and WATER mixed together'. It was this engineering skill which won him a post with Mehemet Ali, Pasha of Egypt, in 1815, thus starting him on a new career as an Egyptologist.

Hardly less popular were exhibitions of automata, whether Rebecqui's Fantoccini in bills of musical and farcical pieces drawn from the regular theatre repertory, or Maillardet's Animated Rope-Dancer whose display provided the thrills without the human concern attendant on a live show. By way of contrast, Mrs Siddons set a coming fashion in entertainments by giving Readings from Shakespeare and Milton for two nights at York House, Clifton. Most of the popular shows were given in the Taylors' Hall, but the area was even then not a good one, and as early as July 1807 James Bannister, arriving in Bristol to give his famous entertainment, *Bannister's Budget, or, An Actor's Ways and Means*, felt he had to apologise 'for his not being able to accommodate his audience in a more commodious room'.

At this period, too, we have some traces of amateur dramatics again. The Bristol Library has two bills of 1806 for 'the Private Theatre, Bristol' set out in close imitation of the professionals, and including in the cast the name of Mr Estlin, later a highly respected civic figure. Less respectable were the adherents of spouting clubs, mainly in the St James's area, whose leading actors were liable to be arrested in mid-performance, when 'the audience . . . immediately dispersed in all directions, and the curtain (*alias coalsacks*) dropped forever.' (*Mirror*, 3.6.1809)

The position of the Theatre Royal in the entertainment pattern of the city began to change quite sharply after the death of William Wyatt Dimond in 1812. His share in the management passed to his ne'er-do-well son William, a writer of cheap popular melodramas, who lived in London and cared nothing for either the Bath or Bristol Theatre except as a source of income. At the same time the gradual national swing towards a stricter public morality became apparent in Bristol—naturally enough in a city which had always contained influential numbers of Quakers and Nonconformists. The newer journals, particularly the Radical *Bristol Mercury* and the moderate *Bristol Mirror*, began to print an increasing number of jibes against management, actors, repertoire and audience, culminating in a virtual boycott for long periods between 1812 and 1815. The Fairs, too, came under persistent attack: the Vicar of Temple had to insist on an apology from one anonymous correspondent who claimed that the revenue from the stands went, not to the poor (as the Vicar had claimed in extenuation of Temple Fair), but into the Vicar's own pocket.

It was during this period that the first direct challenge to the Theatre Royal arose, as a result of the lively commercialism of one Walter Jenkins, a broker. In 1810 he took over the Assembly Rooms, which had hitherto been used almost entirely for concerts, and in the summer of 1811 refurbished and rearranged them so that they might serve as a dining hall, concert room or theatre; he then naturally looked round to see what further honest penny he could turn with them. More fashionably sited and appreciably larger than the Taylors' Hall, the Rooms, provocatively rechristened The New Theatre, would hold 600 in the Boxes and Gallery and 900 in the Pit, and the first theatrical clients were Charles Incledon and the elder Charles Mathews in their two-man entertainment *The Travellers*, for which they wisely sought the permission of the Mayor. This was in November 1811; in January 1812 Masquerade Balls were advertised, then cancelled; 'ENTERTAINMENTS entirely new' were promised, but turned out to be acrobatic and rope displays by Wilson and Sieur Harnn Michalets Sanches, who had appeared with Bannister's Circus back in 1806, and for whom the building was renamed the Regency Theatre.

Rivalry with the Royal, however, did not begin till August 1812, when Lawler, who had been with Elliston at the Surrey Theatre, opened the Regency for light theatrical fare during the Royal's summer closure.

The Entertainments that are to be produced, will combine Grandeur, Interest, and Comic Effect; but never departing from the strictest line of decorum. The more juvenile part of society will find in them that entertainment which they could not derive from the regular Drama, intended for the gratification of the mature and expanded mind; yet they will be sufficiently rational to agreeably amuse the adult, and occasionally be made the humble instrument of celebrating the glorious victories of our army and navy. (*Felix Farley's Bristol Journal*, 15.8.1812)

The manager's first notion of juvenile entertainment was a piece alarmingly called *The Monk and the Murderer, or, Blood will have Blood!* but the accent was on dancing and pantomime, and Lawler and his successor, Clarke from Exeter, drew good audiences. They even managed to lure away from the Theatre Royal Stock Company Bristol's favourite Clown, Bob Gomery.

Perhaps this was the last straw for the theatre managers; at any rate, despite the fact that the Regency deliberately avoided play nights as far as possible, Charlton put it to the Theatre Royal proprietors that the performances were 'extremely injurious to their interests' (not to mention illegal), and between them they arranged an 'information' which put the leading man, John Betterton, into gaol on the eve of his Benefit. This action not surprisingly succeeded only in rousing considerable sympathy—and a bumper Benefit—for Betterton, and long-lasting animus against the Theatre Royal.

It was very foolish of the proprietors to allow themselves to be stampeded in this way, for the Regency, despite its popularity, was really a rather tatty concern, riven with feuds and only spasmodically effective. A patriotic piece 'on the late Glorious Atchievement [*sic*] of Earl Wellington' was recurrently advertised but never performed; and the equestrian statue built for the serious pantomime of *Don Juan* proved when it came to the point to be too big to go through the prop-room doorway, a debacle which had to be hastily explained away by Betterton.

Internal squabbles, rather than the vindictiveness of the Theatre Royal management, closed the Regency in March 1813. In August West & Woolford's Equestrian Company performed hippodramas (melodramas featuring trained horses) at the Royal, leaving Bristol just before Adams arrived, with a troop including the young Ducrow, for the September Fair. Then in mid-November Adams advertised that he had taken the Regency, and intended 'to open it IN A FEW DAYS, with a Grand Display of HORSEMANSHIP, BURLETTA, and PANTOMIME PERFORMANCES, and a Variety of other AMUSEMENTS', but whether he ever performed there is uncertain—though there is trace of an otherwise unidentified 'New Equestrian Circus' in January 1814 with ballets and a tight-rope display by Ducrow.

While this somewhat unedifying contest was going on, Bristolians were not without other amusements. Moritz, Adams, Powell and West & Woolford were fairly regular circus visitors at the Fairs, together with Polito's and Miles's Menageries; Philipstal and Maillardet brought a Mechanical Museum to the Assembly Rooms in March 1811 and stayed for two months, ending with phantasmagorial effects:

a Specteorlogical [sic] Display of various grotesque, fanciful Apparitions, and interesting Characters, will be introduced during a tremendous Storm of Thunder and Lightning; Amongst which will appear the immortal and lamented Hero, the late LORD NELSON, crowned by Fame in the Arms of Victory, &c. (*Bristol Mirror*, 11.5.1811)

Madame Tussaud brought her Collection of Figures to the Assembly Rooms for the first time of many to come in August 1814.

The type of reading pioneered by Mrs Siddons now became more popular; Sarah Smith recited parts of *Paradise Lost* at Mangeon's Hotel, Clifton, in April 1813, and Mrs Beverly, a prepossessing young lady, gained distinguished patronage for her Olios (medleys of songs and recitations) on a number of visits in 1815 and 1816 until she was arrested in Birmingham in September 1816 and convicted of pilfering a handkerchief. Incledon and Mathews continued to contribute miscellanies of song and patter in the earlier tradition.

The post-war economic decline and the stiffening in moral attitudes were certainly factors in the falling-off in support of the Theatre Royal; but a cheapening of repertoire, a decline in acting standards, and above all the petty tyranny of the proprietors and Managers as displayed towards the Regency, made appreciable contributions. The Bath Company's lease of the Royal ran out in the summer of 1817, and after some not very creditable manoeuvring, the theatre was let to John Boles Watson junior, of the Cheltenham and Gloucester theatres; a shifty near-bankrupt, whose management collapsed in less than a year. For nine more months the theatre stayed closed, by which time the prestige and popularity built up over the past 50 years had been almost totally dissipated.

The Assembly Rooms now housed a variety of entertainments outside the Fairs: concerts, a representation of Princess Charlotte's lying-in-state, Charles Mathews' Mail Coach Adventures, the Two Wonderful Russian Fireproof Phenomena, and Clara Fisher's Lilliputian Company of child actors in extracts from *Jane Shore* and *Richard III*—that apparently irresistible lure to infant prodigies of both sexes. Interspersed with these was a sudden mania for boxing matches at both the Taylors' Hall and Assembly Rooms.

It may have been this development which led William M'Cready the elder, who took over management of the Royal in March 1819 at the age of 64, to address the citizens of Bristol in these terms:

It is yet problematical, whether in Bristol the Stage shall preserve its legitimate appropriation to the representation of our divine Shakespeare's works, and to the exercise of our first actors' talents,—or whether it shall be converted into an arena for the display of Pugilistic Contests, and the low senseless mummeries, by which (falling into the hands of inexperienced and grasping adventurers) it must eventually be disgraced and polluted.

Managerial prospectuses have much in common with election manifestoes, especially when it comes to carrying them out. M'Cready did indeed produce some remarkable Stock Company revivals of Shakespeare, notably *A Winter's Tale, Julius Caesar* and *Richard II*, quite apart from providing backing for visiting stars like his son William Charles Macready, Edmund Kean and Junius Brutus Booth; he also had an excellent record in staging eighteenth-century classics. But he had to survive commercially, and to do this he was happily willing in practice to follow the divine Shakespeare's works by *Tom and Jerry, or, Life in London* (complete with pugilistic contests), and to engage any attraction from a puppet show to an opera company.

At Fair times and at Christmas the entertainments in the way of acrobats, jugglers, pantomimists and dioramic effects rivalled the travelling showmen; horses, dogs, cats, and even more miscellaneous fauna (live and manufactured) were to be seen, not only in booths and inn-rooms, but on the Theatre Royal stage. An 1822 pantomime had 'a Stupendous SERPENT or BOA-CONSTRICTOR pursuing a BUTTERFLY, producing an effect hitherto unknown in this country', while a week later there were '*Two Stupendous Serpents*, or, BOA-CONSTRICTORS, each pursuing a BUTTERFLY, In opposite directions, producing A BRILLIANT EFFECT, *NEVER ATTEMPTED BY ANY OTHER ARTIST*.' The previous year M'Cready had staged a 'Historical Melo-Dramatic Entertainment' called *The Egyptian Tomb*, displaying a full-scale reproduction of Belzoni's discovery at Abu Simbel as recreated (appropriately) in the Egyptian Hall, Piccadilly. This antedated by four years what might be termed the touring version of Belzoni's exhibition, which was brought to the St James's Fair of 1825, two years after Belzoni's death, and quite eclipsed the showman's Egyptian Mummy, 'entirely unwrapped as far as Propriety will permit'.

It is impossible not to respond to M'Cready, both as a personality and as a manager. Rushing on with a bucket of water to douse the leading man's wig which had caught fire by the untimely explosion of a firework; apologising profusely for the failure of his newly-installed gas light while the audience sang God Save the King; quarrelling furiously with the Bristol press over adverse criticisms of his actors; he was always his unselfconscious, irascible, exuberant self, and if his company were often infuriated by his temperamental outbursts, many paid generous tribute to the practical knowledge of their craft which they learned from him. M'Cready was a Victorian before Victoria, in his paternalism, his business application, and his public morality. He was a highly-respected Freemason and at his death was buried, like Powell, in Bristol Cathedral; such a pillar of probity, in fact, that it comes as a shock to discover that his leading lady, Sarah Desmond, had been his mistress for at least eight years before he married her in 1821, at which date they had a seven-year old son, passed off as M'Cready's nephew.

If M'Cready showed himself unconcerned about artistic distinctions in his theatrical engagements, his competitors for their part were rapidly losing any particular respect for the position of the Theatre Royal. There was no longer any question of avoiding play-nights, for these were now four or five a week for at least six months of the year, and included the periods of both Charter Fairs. More halls were coming into regular use for entertainment, such as the Great Room at 50 Wine Street; in the mid-1820s a building opposite the Drawbridge on St Augustine's Back was fitted up as a tiny theatre-cum-exhibition room known, rather flatteringly, as the Gallery of Arts. This was used by such various entertainers as the Chevalier Bettes with his Fantoccini, panorama showmen, and another of the innumerable infant prodigies, Master Burton—even, in 1835, for Signor Bertoletto's Extraordinary Exhibition of the Industrious Fleas.

Individual entertainers in ones and twos supplemented dramatic fare by their shows; not only actors like Charles Mathews and Frederick Yates, who were national names, but numerous lesser figures: jugglers, conjurors and ventriloquists, such as Mons. Alexandre who rather engagingly advertised that 'being a Native of *Paris*, it is hoped *French Leave* will be granted to any Peculiarities of Pronunciation of the English Language that may be *found absent*.' At Fair times illuminated booths were often advertised; the performers therein much less often declared themselves, or were reported by the press, though the *Bristol Mirror* described how at the 1825 St James's Fair

We heard the trumpet-tongued Manager of one of the Theatres boast that he is under the special patronage of his Majesty, 'who has graciously sent him,' said the Manager, 'to travel in the provinces for the amusement of his loving subjects!' Scowton's Theatre shines in all the pomp of crimson draperies and variegated lamps . . .

National and international history and geography were painlessly taught by the numerous panoramas, dioramas and models visiting both at Fair times and outside. One of the best-known mechanical exhibitions was Thiodon's Mechanical Theatre of Arts—for which the owner once neglected to apply for civic permission and barely scraped by without prosecution. The Maffeys made no such mistake in 1826 when showing their Theatre of the Petit Lazary:

COMEDIES, PANTOMIMES, FAIRY TALES, &c., performed by Figures, two feet high . . . Messrs. MAFFEY respectfully inform the Inhabitants of this City that their Performances combine morality with instruction and amusement, and can be visited by the most scrupulous. (*Bristol Mercury*, 20.5.1826)

It was in this decade that circus proprietors began to work towards having once again a permanent site in the city. Perhaps encouraged by his success in hippodramas at the Theatre Royal, Ducrow adapted a Riding School in Portwall Lane for a month's season, out of fair time, late in 1825. Ryan, who had taken over Adams's troupe, fitted up his own Olympic Circus in Panting's timber-yard in Lower Montague Street, alongside St James's Churchyard, in August 1826, and stayed till November, despite the renewed competition of Ducrow at the Theatre Royal. In August 1827 Ryan was back constructing a new and better Arena on the same site:

This extensive BUILDING, being 100 feet in length, by nearly 60 feet in width, will be Brilliantly Illuminated with Gas, superbly and tastefully ornamented by one of the first Artists in Bristol. Containing Front Boxes —Side Boxes—good Pit—and a spacious Gallery, which have been judiciously laid out, that every class of persons will find themselves safe and secure, without a possibility of being interrupted from one place to the other. Also, an entrance being separate to each place, the higher and better Orders need no alarm in visiting this fashionable Place of Amusement, where the Performances will be found chaste and highly finished. (*Bristol Gazette*, 23.8.1827)

For five years all told Ryan used this site during the September Fair, advertising larger and better-lit buildings every year.

The blurring of distinctions between the fare offered by the Theatre Royal and by other sources of entertainment, and the strengthened independence of non-theatrical entrepreneurs, apparent during old M'Cready's management, grew greater after his death in 1829. The management of his successor, Richard Brunton, collapsed in bankruptcy after two years; a brief re-union with Bath fared no better, the Bath Theatre being in even worse straits than that of Bristol; while the Bristol Riots of 1831 brought devastation to a locality which was already becoming seedy. The artistic and political chaos of the four years after M'Cready's death destroyed much of the goodwill he had been at such pains to re-establish during his ten years at the helm.

Finally his widow, Sarah M'Cready, took the theatre lease in 1834, though with not much more than sentimental sympathy to support her. She faced circumstances in every way depressing; recurrent outbreaks of cholera, for example, during one of which the Rackhay, a festering slum at the back of the theatre, was swept by the disease, and its inhabitants looked out of their windows on to a newly-reopened graveyard to see their neighbours' bodies being brought out for interment. On that occasion Mrs M'Cready dared not open the theatre for six months.

The recession in trade, the running-down of the theatre building itself as well as of its environs, the general upheaval in the provincial theatre and uncertainty in that of the metropolis, coupled with her total lack of personal capital, all militated against the success of Mrs M'Cready's enterprise. William M'Cready had finally made his way by his unquenchable, Micawber-like ebullience; Sarah could only cling on grimly and survive by concentrated application and a quite illogical courage. It is infinitely to her credit that in 20 of the most difficult years in provincial theatre history she kept going indomitably, paid her rent and her actors even though it emptied her own purse, and preserved a continuity of management which was invaluable when at last the tide began to turn.

But the lack of material resources left her much more vulnerable to competition, especially from the circuses, than any of her predecessors. In December 1832 Ducrow had obtained a licence for a new National Olympic Arena, erected in North Street to the design of his tame architect Atkins, which was used by Ryan in 1833 and subsequent years. Here the nearby Full Moon Inn provided useful stabling facilities and accommodation for artists; and the site, as the *Bristol Gazette* shrewdly observed, 'though out of the noise of the Fair itself, is sufficiently near to prevent visitors having to travel out of their way.' (*Bristol Gazette*, 5.9.1833).

The permanent building Ryan finally erected on this site in 1837, and which nearly bankrupted him, remained till almost the end of the century, latterly as a Salvation Army Citadel, its dome a landmark in the area till it burned down in 1895. An advertisement in the *Bristol Mercury* of 20 July 1839 described it rapturously:

This Superior Edifice is supported by 42 square columns, and calculated to hold, seated, with a good view of the stage and circle, 2000 spectators. The BOXES—Dress, Upper, and Side—are all covered with cloth of soft texture. The PIT—Commodious and well aired. The GALLERY—Large, and peculiarly adapted for seeing, hearing, and comfort. The CIRCLE— The most capacious in England. . . The STAGE—Built for the display of scenic illusions, processions over lofty bridges, combats, horse and foot. Spectacles, Melo-Drama, Comic Pantomimes, and grand Operatic Ballets.

Besides this Arena, Price and Powell put up a New Circus Royal less than a quarter of a mile away on the corner of Milk Street and Barr Street, and in the Spring of 1842 both circuses were in full swing. This had such a depressing effect on theatre attendances that Mrs M'Cready had to close her season a month early.

Moreover as the general movement towards a free stage grew, so entertainers of all kinds enlarged their scope and took more risks with the material they included in their shows. Again, it was the circuses which sailed nearest to the wind; though they left full-length hippo-dramas to engagements at the Theatre Royal, in their arenas they progressed from costumed processions and short burlettas to the Grand Equestrian and Pedestrian Spectacle, *St George and the Dragon*; and *The Idiot Witness, or, The Queen's Page of the Sixteenth Century*, during which 'various interesting situations and effects occur, particularly the grand and impressive Equestrian Tableaux of Queen Elizabeth's Court at Greenwich'. This was in 1839; the following year Ryan was so blatant in his inclusion of dramatic material that the Theatre Royal Proprietors had to take a very threatening line with his local manager, Usher (the former Clown of the Coburg—later Old Vic—Theatre), and he shut up shop for that season; but the long-term effects were negligible.

Ryan's Circus—as it continued to be called long after Ryan's only connection with it was limited to a charitable Benefit given by other visiting proprietors—was also used for a multiplicity of entertainments from Masquerades to Cornish Wrestling, but primarily it provided a focal point for the touring equestrian companies of Ducrow, Batty,

Cornwall, Hughes and Cooke, and also played host to some eminent foreign troupes: Tourniaire's, Franconi's and Macarte's in particular. Tenting circuses used the adjacent Moon Fields or occasionally ventured into the expanding village of Clifton, where at the top of Park Street the Horticultural Gardens housed at various times Macarte and Bell's Circus, Van Amburgh's performing animals, and even a peculiar venture into pantomime and *poses plastiques* run by Mr and Mrs R. Power, late of the Theatre Royal, Bristol.

Staple popular entertainments continued as before: jugglers, conjurors, menageries, freaks, instructive panoramas. The Saloon of Bridge House, Drawbridge, was occupied for a month in 1838 by Rebecqui's Fantoccini, in which were incorporated the puppets which had belonged to that stalwart of the eighteenth-century showgrounds, Seward. These were said to be 'free from the unsightly appendage of Tin Tubes, extending from the head upwards, as visible in Maffey's and other Spectacles des Marionettes' and were able 'to traverse the Stage in every direction, advancing and receding, according to circumstances, without visible agency'. (*Bristol Mirror*, 28.4.1838.) Among new developments there was a rage for Scottish and Irish entertainments, and the establishment of Bank Holiday fêtes at the Zoological Gardens. Since these fund-raising galas incorporated outdoor entertainments, a band for dancing, and a final firework display, they must have been extremely upsetting for the animals. The choice of attractions was sometimes surprising: the engagement of Van Amburgh with his lions and elephant in July 1839 surely represents a classic case of carrying coals to Newcastle.

During Mrs M'Cready's management the Pleasure Fairs, which had been under attack for many years, were finally abolished. The proximate cause of the moralists' success was the sensational murder of Mrs Mary Lewis, mother-in-law of one Samuel Charles Bartlett, a strolling player, in 1836. Bartlett, leading man of Ingleton's Sans Pareil Company at the St James's Fair, was accused of shooting her for a pitifully small bequest which might have enabled him to set up in independent management. The accounts of the inquest and trial contain fascinating glimpses of the life in these travelling shows. Here is some of the evidence given by 16-year-old Henry Lovell, whom Bartlett had sent to get ammunition for his pistol:

There was a rival show of a similar kind erected close beside Ingleton's; on Mr. Ingleton's front stage you could converse with a person standing on Mr. Middleton's front stage. . . There is a great deal of noise made at these shows by drums, trumpets, shouting, and firing off fire-arms. Noise is one of the means made use of to draw attention to the performers; when the public hear a drum beating at one place, and a louder noise at another, they sometimes go to the loudest of them. . . (*Bristol Mercury*, 9.4.1837, which contains an almost verbatim account of the trial.)

The evidence against Bartlett was entirely circumstantial but overwhelming. By macabre coincidence, at the moment the Judge was pronouncing sentence of death, Bartlett's wife was giving birth to a still-born child.

If this were not enough, in the next Fair the strollers were actually giving a dramatised version of 'the lamentable tragedy of Lippet's lane, or the inhuman murder of his mother-in-law, by Bartlett'. Lord George Sanger, in his *Seventy Years a Showman*, has a garbled account of the tragedy, and he describes in vivid terms the popular reaction against 'the play-actors who killed the poor old woman'. It is little wonder that, capitalising on the wave of revulsion, the moralists were able to get the Pleasure Fairs suppressed in 1838.

This suppression, however, proved no help to the legitimate theatre. Quite apart from the inevitable indiscriminate backlash of the lurid scandal, it meant that showmen and entertainers had now no particular reason to concentrate their visits within specific periods; any time of year was now as good as another.

In addition, a new local competitor to the theatre began to arise in the 1840s, the tavern music hall. Its heyday in Bristol was not till the next decade, but already in January 1845 James Doughty was advertising the success of his Cider House off Broad Street, and his engagement of 'Mr J. Freer, the great nondescript Singer, from the Glasgow and London Concerts'. The Concert Room was open from 7 to 11, and no women or boys were to be admitted.

Doughty is one of the most intriguing characters in the history of Bristol entertainment. In 1838 we find him as a minor actor on the Theatre Royal stage, alongside the young Dion Boucicault; he reappears as a Clown in circus after circus in Bristol; in November 1854 he introduced the youthful Louisa Herbert, later manageress of the St James's Theatre in London, to the local stage; and his act with performing dogs was incorporated in a Theatre Royal pantomime of 1862. This act was seen in Brighton 45 years later by Sybil Thorndike and Lewis Casson during the days of their engagement when Doughty must have been about 85; he died in 1913, somewhere in his nineties, working almost to the last.

His was the most successful Concert Room of the period, and gave a start to the Great Mackney, for one. However, it was not long before the London Oyster Rooms in High Street, and the Post Office Tavern and the Beaufort Rooms, both in Broad Street, were following suit. This area, a honeycomb of courts and passages, bordering some of the most notorious 'rookeries' of Bristol in St James's Back and the Pithay, was to become the centre of gaffs and concert halls of the cheapest kind.

To meet the requirements of rather more respectable forms of entertainment, other public halls were being built at this period, the most important being the Victoria Rooms, opened in 1842 to serve the polite and moneyed Clifton area. This speedily attracted most of the good concert artists, many entertainers, actors giving play-readings, and even some theatrical companies like Dickens's Amateur Company of the Guild of Literature and Art, who had reckoned that their prices would be too much for the Theatre Royal's usual audience. As their tickets cost about three times those at the Royal, they were probably right.

Other halls opening about this time were the Broadmead Rooms (started by followers of Robert Owen as a Hall of Science in 1840), and the small Royal Albert Rooms in College Green. Artists can be found moving from one hall to another, or to the Theatre Royal, as opportunity offered; the increase in the number of halls is proof of the growth of appetite for novelty and popular entertainment of all kinds. Though Mrs M'Cready brought most of the great stars of classical drama, opera and ballet to her theatre, she could not neglect any engagement which might bring in an audience, from rope-dancers to performing animals, from Herr Michael Boai who played tunes on his chin to troupes of Ethiopian Serenaders; in a growing city there was an increasing clientèle among lower middle-class and working people for whom all the managements were competing.

This uneasy, and from the Theatre Royal's point of view ultimately destructive, state of affairs continued throughout Mrs M'Cready's lesseeship. As she grew older she became less and less able to do more than keep the place going from one penny-pinching week to the next, and the addition of the bankrupt Theatre Royal, Bath, to the circuit in 1845 proved as much of an embarrassment as a help. In her last years she had her resourceful and enterprising son-in-law, James Henry Chute, as lieutenant, and when on her death in the spring of 1853 Chute took over the lease, there was something like a revolution in the repertoire and whole aim of the Theatre Royal, and consequently of its relation with popular entertainments.

Between Dimond's retirement from the stage in 1801 and Mrs M'Cready's death, however, the pattern of amusements in Bristol was one of developing and constantly modifying interaction. The day of the purist was to come.

FOUR

From Music Hall to Movies

1853–1901

Under James Henry Chute the Theatre Royal became once more the recognised training ground for the future London star. A number of the leading figures of the late Victorian stage, including Kate and Ellen Terry, Marie Wilton, Madge Robertson, William and George Rignold and Charles Coghlan, gained much of their early stage experience under Chute, and hardly a West End bill of the last quarter of the century lacked at least one name familiar to Bristol playgoers.

This remarkable achievement was due primarily to Chute's blend of courage, idealism and shrewd commercial acumen. In the autumn recess of 1853 he spent the best part of £1,000 on vital repairs and redecoration of the theatre; he reopened with a series of prestige re-productions of Charles Kean's elaborate Shakespearean revivals at the Princess's; and thereafter tempted his audience with carefully mounted Christmas pantomime, burlesque, classics and sensation dramas in turn. Firmly and deliberately he cut away the accretions of popular entertainment in his main seasons: let music hall artistes go to the music halls, animal acts and acrobats to the circuses, and never mind if they mounted an equestrian version of *Uncle Tom's Cabin* or a rival panto-mime on the Valentine and Orson legend during the same Christmas season—this was not the audience he wanted.

Respectability of audience and of programme was one of Chute's great aims, but united with what may now suggest priggishness was a far higher concept than that held by most contemporary managers of the place theatre should have in the artistic and, as Chute would have added, the moral and educational life of a city. Benevolently paternalistic, he encouraged the members of his company to break out of the prevalent strait-jacket of type-casting, and raised the standards of teamwork till he could, like his eighteenth-century predecessors, be independent of so-called stars.

While Chute was creating his Temple of the Drama, caterers for popular tastes were equally busy. Tavern music halls sprang up all over the old centre of the city during the 1850s. Broad Street and its courts were still the centre of this activity; in Cider House Passage alone there were Doughty's, the Raglan Tavern and the Reform. Among their rivals were the Canterbury in Maryleport Street, the Ship and Castle (later City Music Hall) in Marsh Street near the junction with Baldwin Street, the Rose Inn in Temple Street and the New Apollo in Queen Street near Bristol Bridge. There were two in King Street itself, the Britannia at the Welsh Back end, and the Old Duke a few doors down, the latter still in existence with its sign now bearing the lineaments of a modern Duke, Duke Ellington, in pleasant adaptation to its present style of musical evenings.

Many of these public houses provided little more than free-and-easy 'convivials' with singing and drinking; admission was often free, the proprietor making his profit on the sale of drink. Women were generally barred—indeed, the 'stag' character was doubtless among the attractions. Other more ambitious proprietors provided a varied programme and some attempt at stage facilities, charging 3d or 6d admission. A typical tavern hall of this kind, possibly the Raglan, was described vividly by a reporter in the *Bristol Times* of 3 February 1855;

We went down a court and up a ricketty pair of stairs into an oblong room, with a wing on the left, as you entered. The place was fitted up with forms with backs, and stands on the top of the backs for glasses, &c. It was crowded with men and women, boys and girls—some of the latter did not appear to be more than 14 or 15 years old. . . At the upper end of the room was a small and primitive stage, with a curtain of paint and canvas in the front, and green baize on the right; the former pulled up like a window blind, the latter was pulled along like a bed-curtain. On the left-hand side of the stage, which, being close to the wall, needed no curtain, was a grand piano, played by a man with a very shiny hat on; he was accompanied by another individual with his hat off. . .

Here the reporter sat through a comic duet, a ventriloquial act, patriotic songs and a series of *poses plastiques* or living statues.

While singers, comic or serious, were the backbone of every bill, dancers, 'negro delineators', performing animals and jugglers were frequent, and one inn even offered a dancing contest between ten wooden-legged men. In the larger halls something in the way of spectacle might also be attempted. At the time of a sensational local murder in October 1857, the manager of the Canterbury was condemned by the *Bristol Gazette* for presenting at his 'dancing-shop in Maryportstreet, what he calls a "splendid Diorama" of the Leigh Woods tragedy, with Charlotte Pugsley laid out with her throat cut, and Mr. Beale [the murderer] making off with her bonnet and shawl'. With some sharpness the manager enquired in the next *Bristol Mercury:* 'Would the Editor explain the difference between exhibiting paintings, and printing as he does in his journal, all the particulars of the Murder?'

Accompanying the growth of the tavern music hall was a proliferation of one-man shows, particularly at the Broadmead Rooms and the rather more select Athenaeum in Corn Street; the recitals of national songs, programmes of sketches and conjuring displays of the 1840s, while not disappearing, now had competition from entertainments by established local actors. Many members of the Theatre Royal Company added usefully to their income out of season by working up an evening's programme. George Melville recited *Hamlet* and *Macbeth* from memory; the young Marie Wilton and her even younger sisters gave glees, choruses, imitations and dramatic extracts. Probably the most ingenious was 'General' Eugene O'Reilly, a popular comic actor, who celebrated his retirement by organising himself a Benefit at the Salutation Inn, out at Henbury, advertising 'The Battle of Waterloo', and offering 'Special Despatch Steamers up the Trym every ten minutes'—a mode of transport which would astonish anyone who looks at that narrow, chuckling little stream today.

Not all these shows were successful. An evening given by one Herr Sablotny, guitarist and singer, 'was cut short, soon after the conclusion of the first part, by the appearance on the platform of the Herr's principal assistant' who accused Frau Sablotny of absconding with the night's receipts, promised for the payment of his own salary arrears; he thereupon refused to finish the performance, 'leaving the unfortunate minstrel of the Tyrolese surrounded by his bill-sticker, his printer, &c., all urgent for payment of their "little accounts".' (*Bristol Mercury*, 3.5.1856)

The talent from the music halls spread over into many types of entertainment. The fêtes at the Zoological Gardens featured a variety of artists, including, on one occasion, Blondin on the tight rope; the proprietor of the Avonmouth Hotel and Gardens actually built a music hall in the grounds; while the Pear Tree Gardens in North Street, Bedminster, and the Horfield Pleasure Gardens copied their better-established rivals as well as they could. The last-named contrived for a short time so successfully to undercut the Zoo in bidding for the patronage of charity fêtes, that a good deal of feeling was aroused, fomented by troublemakers who exaggerated some minor police charges into accusations of wholesale misbehaviour and immorality. Ultimately its site on the northern outskirts of the city told against it, and after passing through several managements and titles it failed, the grounds being sold—doubtless to the self-satisfaction of its opponents—as the site of the present Horfield Gaol.

The 'delineators of negro character' of the music halls proved precursors of a new but allied type of entertainment, the Christy Minstrel show. The rage for these blackface shows with their set comic, musical and dance routines swept the country in the 1850s and continued with variations to the end of the century; even Chute gave engagements to one or two of the leading companies at slack periods of the season. Individual London music hall artists began to make up small touring companies of their own, and booked public halls: Sam Cowell, The Great Mackney, Jolly John Nash from Gloucestershire and Harry Clifton were among the most popular in Bristol, appearing usually at the Broadmead Rooms, but occasionally penetrating into Clifton for an engagement at the Victoria Rooms.

Most often the Victoria Rooms specialised in entertainments designed for the more moneyed and leisured families who were increasingly moving into the growing suburbs of Clifton and Redland in northwest Bristol. Charles Dickens gave readings from his works there in 1866, 1867 and 1869; established actresses like Isabella Glyn, Mrs Scott Siddons (Sarah's great-grand-daughter) and Amy Sedgwick gave dramatic recitals; and it was the recurrent home of Mr and Mrs German Reed's Drawing Room Entertainments of songs and sketches, continued by Corney Grain and Rutland Barrington after the Reeds had died. The pull of the Clifton audience is similarly attested by the gradual migration of the larger circuses from the old St James's Fair neighbourhood to the Rifle Drill Hall at the top of Park Street, on the present University Refectory site.

This was the audience which Chute wanted—and needed from the financial point of view—to secure for his Theatre Royal, but in spite of the many tributes to his personal probity and ability Clifton was apparently reluctant to make the steep descent down Park Street to the admittedly slummy purlieus of King Street. The Bath Theatre Royal continued to prove a losing concern for Chute despite its replacement, only twelve months after a disastrous fire in 1862, by an up-to-date building which made the Bristol theatre appear a very sorry contrast. Hints, advice, even detailed proposals for new sites and organisation were not lacking; Chute ignored them all until he was ready.

In October 1866 Chute bought a site on the south side of Park Row, near the top of Park Street and therefore easily accessible both from Bristol and Clifton. A year later, on 14 October 1867, he was able to open his New Theatre Royal, designed by the prolific theatre architect C. J. Phipps. It seated over 2,100 in pit stalls and pit, lower and upper balconies and gallery, and had every appliance for staging spectacle which Victorian ingenuity furnished. Indeed, Chute added some inventions of his own, including 'a novel form of mediums for the float [foot] lights of coloured glass revolving on cylinders round the lights, so that by means of a lever at the prompter's box the change can be made from white to red or green lights in an instant'. He had always a particular interest in developments in stage-lighting and made numerous experiments with the new limelight and even newer electricity during his management.

Chute, who had suffered considerably as lessee of the King Street Theatre from the hostility of one of the leading proprietors, was determined to be his own master in Park Row, and raised the money—estimated at £12,000 but ultimately reported as over £18,000—from personal resources and by short-term loans. He intended originally to keep both Bristol theatres and the Theatre Royal, Bath in operation, but this proved an impossible financial strain; he nearly went bankrupt in 1868. He gave up the Bath lease in that year with some relief, while after the pantomime season of 1867–8 the King Street Theatre was opened only at irregular intervals, becoming little more than an overflow theatre. Its attractions, when they were available, ranged as widely as in Mrs M'Cready's day, from the intimate comedies of T. W. Robertson to the broad music-hall songs of Vance, Arthur Lloyd, G. H. Macdermott and Jolly John Nash; and from Grand Opera to the South Carolina Female Minstrels. The Theatre Royal was even let out on Sundays for evangelical services, suitable ecclesiastical scenery forming a background for those officiating on the stage.

Part of Chute's difficulty lay in the state of transition in the theatre as a whole at that period. An uneasy position had been reached in which a purely local Stock Company was becoming regarded as old-fashioned, but there were not as yet enough independent touring attractions to fill up the year, and Chute, like other provincial managers, found himself in danger of falling between two stools. A further blow, both economic and personal, came on Boxing Night (27 December) of 1869. Huge pit and gallery queues were waiting side by side on the down gradient leading to the entrances of the New Theatre Royal, to see the pantomime. Pressure built up so intolerably that, when the doors were opened, those in front were pushed over and trampled on by those behind, who were generally unconscious of anything amiss. In all, 18 people were killed and many more hurt in this disaster, and the moral blow to Chute was severe; many friends claimed that he never fully recovered his old *élan*.

Furthermore, it became plain that, as commonly applies, distance from the theatre was an excuse rather than a reason for not attending it. Except on the early nights of some spectacular Shakespeare revival or sensation drama by Falconer or Boucicault, houses were often lamentably thin. Much rested on the success of the pantomime, and here the upsurge of music hall and the rise of opera bouffe drained off many of the best artistes so that Chute was sometimes compelled to make do with what an agent had left on his books. One such was a young woman with an especially strident Cockney twang whom he was forced to engage as Dick Whittington. He comforted himself as best he could with the thought that this, after all, might represent the authentic Dick: 'a boy of the lower order, a *gamin*, born and bred within the sound of Bow Bells'; but his friend Rennie Powell thought he detected a certain volcanic rumbling beneath the words.

Clinging to the old values, Chute kept a Stock Company going till his death in 1878; his sons, James and George Macready Chute, changed almost immediately to the touring principle, and three years later gave up the house in King Street. The New Theatre Royal in Park Row established itself as a No. 1 touring theatre of the highest standards, its resident scenic designers often creating special sets for the more important attractions in the days before tons of scenery and properties accompanied the travelling companies.

The New Theatre Royal had from the outset taken away from the 'Old' a great deal of the middle-class audience available for legitimate drama and opera; and there was equally keen competition for other types of audience. Music-hall entertainment rapidly became professionalised and taverns were adapted accordingly. The first Canterbury Music Hall burned down in September 1859, but a new purpose-built hall with a stage, galleries and 'convenient offices' was opened the following year. The Rose Inn was reconstructed as the New Colosseum in 1860. Throughout the 'sixties and 'seventies there was continuous activity, marked by the opening on 12 December 1870 of the Alhambra Music

Hall at 15 Broadmead ('Billiard Saloon and Spirit Vaults Open All Day'). Burned down in 1874 and rebuilt with considerable improvements, it continued under various titles in direct development from its public-house predecessors. F. G. Lewin recalled it 50 years later as resembling a chapel with pews each side of the aisle—but with glasses of beer taking the place of hymn books.

At the top of the aisle in front of the small stage and proscenium, the M.C. posed in an arm chair, before what appeared to be a reading desk, and with a small ivory hammer, of the auctioneer type, he would thump upon his rostrum for silence, as Miss So-and-so was about to appear in her celebrated song and dance. (*Bristol Times and Mirror*, 12.5.1923)

Another popular meeting-place was the Old Globe in Christmas Street, run by Ernee Clarke, music hall singer and popular song writer, where an exclusively male clientèle was promised 'Good Songs, pleasant Company, and the best Liquors procurable, at popular prices'.

There was no falling off in the allure of the circus, which probably had the broadest appeal of any form of entertainment. The North Street building gradually fell into disuse, but nearby sites in the Moon Fields and on a tip in Newfoundland Street were still available. Better still, the Rifle Drill Hall at the top of Park Street had the advantage of a much more salubrious neighbourhood, and could be easily adapted for longer stays by Hengler's, Sanger's or McCollum's companies. Its readily available gas and water supplies enabled them to mount ever more elaborate spectacles with water effects; *Cinderella*, with ponies, was of course a stock attraction, while *Mazeppa* and *Dick Turpin* usually signalled the approach of the last weeks of the season. Almost opposite the New Theatre Royal was a vacant lot on which a quite substantial wooden building was erected by Newsome for circus performances in 1876, and similar arrangements were made by other equestrian troupes; the place even had a short career as a music hall in 1887 under the name of Watson's Circus of Varieties.

Crazes for cycling, skating and spelling-bees came and went; the Colston Halls, the larger of which opened in 1867 for major concerts and mass meetings, were soon hired by minstrels and concert parties, in competition with the Broadmead Rooms and to the total extinction of the old Assembly Rooms.

The diorama took on a new lease of life in the elaborate and genuinely artistic canvases displayed by Hamilton and the Poole Brothers under the title of Myrioramas; in place of the Phantasmagoria, audiences were entertained by magic lantern shows with 'dissolving views'. The best known of these illusions, Pepper's Ghost, was exploited by Spectral Opera Companies, who presented skeletal versions of Gounod's *Faust*, Barnett's *Mountain Sylph* and Dickens's *Christmas Carol*, with emphasis, of course, on the supernatural effects.

There was still entertainment in the streets. One night in January 1870 Clifton Police Station found itself housing two bears, which together with their French keeper and his son had been arrested after an *al fresco* performance which blocked the road. Even greater obstruction was caused in February 1872 by two rival firms on opposite sides of Wine Street, still as narrow and as overhung with shops and houses as in Elizabethan days. In an endeavour to attract attention to themselves and block up the entrance to the other's shop, they hired, respectively, a magic lantern exhibition and a Punch and Judy show for display in their upper windows. No-one, cart-driver or pedestrian, could get through this central thoroughfare for three successive evenings, until police persuasion brought the shop-owners reluctantly to their senses.

There is evidence, too, that the official suppression of the Pleasure Fairs did not result in their total extinction, and certainly did not keep away the strolling players. In St Philip's, a poverty-stricken district just across the river from the old Temple Fair site, the March fair was revived as early as 1854 when there was a 300-ft long Saloon, christened Casino de Venise, 'Illuminated with Three Thousand variegated Lamps'; 'Mr. BAKER's celebrated THEATRICAL COMPANY' was a further attraction. Nearly 30 years later the *Bristol Mercury*, in an influential series of articles on the Homes of the Bristol Poor, described sympathetically Joe Baker's tented Prince of Wales Theatre and his Christmas pantomime of *Aladdin*.

It is true that the magic cave was a modest affair, and the *andante* by the orchestra of two cornets and a trombone required a little softening for weird and eerie effect, and brilliant red fire did a great part in the transformation scene and the Fairies' Home, but the harlequinade, with smart clown, active pantaloon, and graceful columbine, arrayed in diaphanous robes, was bustling enough, and was so full of fun as to provoke roars of laughter. The bright faces of the four hundred Philippians showed that they thoroughly enjoyed their pantomime, which lasted nearly two hours. (*Bristol Mercury*, 31.12.1883)

Apparently Baker was a regular visitor for nearly 40 years, using, like the circuses and menageries, whatever patches of clear ground were available in St Paul's, St Philip's or Bedminster, and though only hints remain, it is clear that unofficial theatres, ranging from the sizeable tented booth of Baker to dangerous candle-lit penny gaffs in deserted shops, went on being set up in Bristol and presumably drawing customers.

All this made it increasingly difficult for the Theatre Royal in King Street to find an audience of its own. When the Chute brothers finally gave up their lease in 1881, they were succeeded by 28-year-old Andrew Melville ('Mr Emm'), son of George Melville who had been a favourite actor at the Royal in the 'fifties and 'sixties. Emm was eccentric, thrusting, outsize in physique and ambitions; leaving his existing South Wales theatres temporarily in his father's care, he poured nearly £5,000 into altering and renovating the Royal, backstage and front, and it is essentially Andrew Melville's Victorianised auditorium and decorations which are to be seen today, though with a Georgian colour scheme superimposed. He cut back the forestage, relaid the stage with every kind of trap, provided new stage doors with niches instead of boxes above, and not least gave us the star-studded ceiling which, against the grey-blue background chosen by Melville, and seen through the shimmer of gas lighting, must have looked even lovelier in 1881 than it does today.

Melville abominated artistic snobbery and possessed a considerable sense of mischief; he loved provoking the Chutes, and it was almost certainly he who instigated the representations which led them in 1884 to abandon the title of New Theatre Royal and rename the Park Row house The Prince's. He was also a professional to his fingertips; on one occasion while he was playing the marooned hero of *The Sea of Ice* in the full glare of green limelight, the tinted glass screen fell off the apparatus and crashed on the stage, leaving him bathed in stark white instead. Not a whit disconcerted, he merely exclaimed: 'Ha! the ice is breaking up!' and strode off the stage. And if his taste was really for farce, melodrama and four-hour pantomimes (in which he himself loved to play a twenty-stone Columbine on Benefit nights), he also gave opportunities at the Theatre Royal to the young Frank Benson with his 'Celebrated Shakesperian and Old English Comedy Company', and to Martin Harvey when with William Haviland and Louis Calvert he first ventured into management.

Unluckily for Bristol, Melville could not rest content with his empire in South Wales and the West; he added other theatres in the Midlands, in Scotland and in Brighton, and without his personal presence and interest, local support as usual dropped away. The situation worsened when Melville contracted diabetes, which in those days was a slow killer, and he finally gave up his lease in 1893.

By this time there had been a number of important changes in the pattern of entertainments. The City Council's belated activities had led to some cleaning up of the slums backing the River Frome in central Bristol, and the small tavern music halls in this area disappeared one by one. The gaffs moved eastwards towards Old Market, concentrating in Castle Street, where old Bristol residents have recalled to me a dozen or more in the 'nineties, from penny theatres to marionette shows. One building which was the subject of particular interest was the former George Inn, 82 Castle Street, a solidly built house with back yard surrounded by stables and warehouses. In November 1886 the Sangers applied to the Society of Merchant Venturers for a lease, intending to adapt it as a circus, but negotiations fell through, and the following year Thomas Baker (possibly a brother to the strolling Joe) was accepted as a yearly tenant.

Baker speedily put the building to use as an entertainment centre: a survey of 28 October 1887 reported that one ground-floor room was used as a Bazaar; behind that was a Concert Hall with gallery ('very ricketty and roughly constructed'), the ceiling 'covered by striped calico material and the walls with paintings on thin canvas'. Adjacent ground-floor rooms were used for boat swings, skittle alleys and other amusements, and on the first floor was a long room 'lately used as a *Running Track* but now as a fitting-up room'.

In December 1888 J. T. Welch applied to lease No. 82 and spend £4,000 in converting it into a large Concert Hall and circus, but would

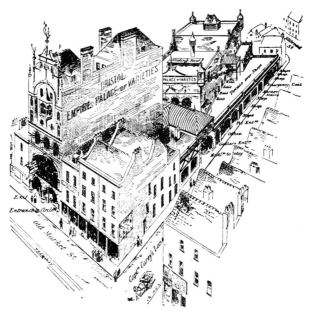

Artist's impression of the Empire Music Hall, Old Market Street, as originally planned in 1891. Reproduced in *Western Daily Press*, 23 August 1954.

The eventual imitation-Moorish frontage of the Empire, opened 1893. *Photograph: Reece Winstone.*

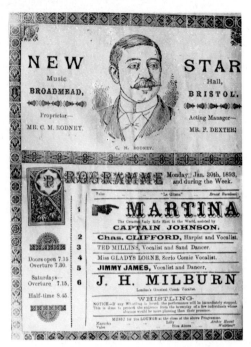

1893 programme of the New Star Music
Hall, Broadmead. *Bristol Reference Library.*

Exterior of the New Theatre Royal (later the Prince's), engraved
for the *Illustrated London News* at the time of the pantomime
disaster, Christmas 1869. *Richard Southern Accession, Theatre
Collection, Bristol University.*

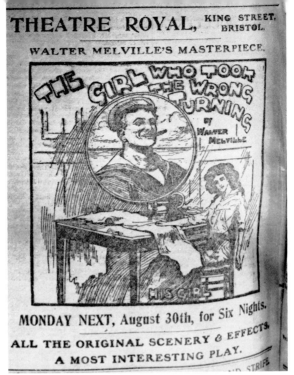

THEATRE ROYAL, KING STREET, BRISTOL.

WALTER MELVILLE'S MASTERPIECE.

THE GIRL WHO TOOK THE WRONG TURNING

BY WALTER MELVILLE

HIS GIRL

MONDAY NEXT, August 30th, for Six Nights.

ALL THE ORIGINAL SCENERY & EFFECTS.

A MOST INTERESTING PLAY.

Melodrama advertisement for the Theatre Royal in 1909. Walter Melville was one of the sons of Andrew Melville, lessee of the Royal from 1881 to 1893. *Western Daily Press*, 28.8.1909.

Stoll's Bristol Hippodrome, opened in 1912, which set new standards for Music Hall. Print supplied by the Management of Bristol Hippodrome.

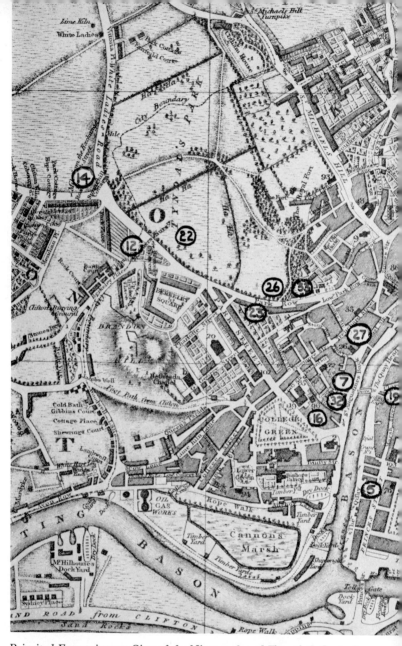

Principal Entertainment Sites of the Nineteenth and Twentieth Centuries

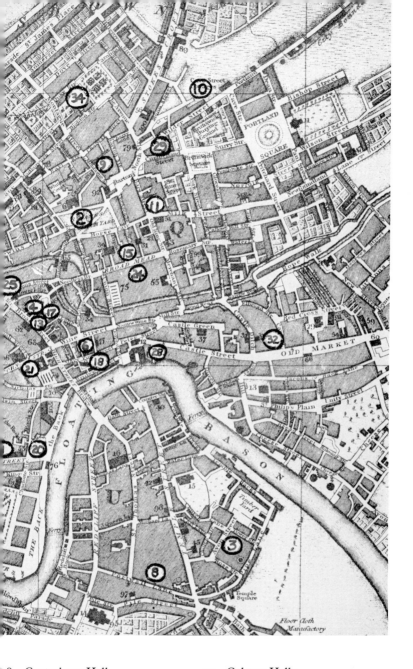

Pastor Manders (Ralph Hutton) rebukes Mrs Alving (Blanche Fothergill) in the first Bristol production of Ibsen's *Ghosts* (described by the *Evening Post* as a 'neurotic sensation drama') at the Little Theatre in March 1937.

Tom Wrench (Ian Richardson) demonstrates to Rose Trelawny (Hayley Mills) a naturalistic touch in his new play under the sympathetic eye of Avonia Bunn (Elizabeth Power). A scene from *Trelawny*, which reopened the Theatre Royal in 1972. *Photograph: Derek Balmer.*

Two aspects of contemporary theatre: social commitment and nostalgia. Top, Tony Robinson (left) and Chris Harris (right) lead Howard Goorney, Tim Fearon and Christine Bradwell in a march through Broadmead to advertise Avon Touring Company's *E (for Environment) Show.* Below, 16-year-old Bristolian, Martin Kay, puts over his Tommy Cooper-type comedy-magic act in Olde Tyme Music Hall at Tiffany's, The Glen. (*Photograph: Whiteladies Photographic Studios.*)

not offer a high enough rent. The following year a more serious attempt was made: Walter Reynolds, a well-known melodrama writer of the time, asked the magistrates for a dramatic licence, proposing to erect a magnificent new theatre on the site. In a massive public-relations campaign he published in the *Bristol Observer* of 18 May 1889 artist's impressions and a section of his proposed 2,500-seat theatre, which was to be convertible into a circus, have a roof garden reached by hydraulic lift, and raise the aesthetic tone of the whole neighbourhood.

Unfortunately there was still a large body of anti-theatre opinion, both clerical and lay, which was amply represented on the magistrates' bench; and in all fairness it must have been difficult for anyone seriously to envisage a second Prince's Theatre in that overcrowded, tough, poverty-ridden area. At any rate, the magistrates refused a licence, and the following year the Merchant Venturers silenced criticism by leasing the building for industrial purposes.

During the 1880s the big circuses finally forsook the St James's area in favour of Park Row, playing either in the Drill Hall or in the fit-up almost opposite the Prince's. Their bills indicated increased appeal to families, the spectacles so theatrical that Sanger actually applied for and was granted a dramatic licence for his production of *Cinderella* in 1882. Tenting circuses had almost disappeared, but menageries were still popular, setting up most often in the Horsefair but also visiting Lawrence Hill and Bedminster, attesting to the spread of the city to the east and south.

A Christmas custom which became rapidly almost as established as the pantomime grew up in the 1880s: the appearance at the Large Colston Hall of one of the Poole Brothers' pictorial Myrioramas, with accompanying concert party. The variety turns were so popular that at one time the Pooles planned to open a music hall in Bristol, for only the little Alhambra (from 1889 known as the New Star) was officially meeting the immense demand for music-hall entertainment.

Indirectly, of course, this entertainment was much more widely available, not only sharing the bill with Myrioramas, but in the form of Concert Parties and Minstrel troupes. The Broadmead Rooms fell into decay, but the Athenaeum in Corn Street, the Lesser Colston Hall, and after September 1885 the St James's Hall in Cumberland Street near the old circus were available and in frequent requisition.

Few such entertainments seem to have come to Clifton, the Victoria Rooms management preferring such fashionable offerings as Oscar Wilde's lectures on aesthetics, dramatic recitals and Maskelyne and Cooke's magic. A new building, the Alexandra Hall in Merchants Road, Clifton, played host to small concerts, recitals and amateur dramatics, though the manager fell foul of the magistrates in 1888 and, unable to obtain a licence, had to restrict his activities thereafter.

The last two decades of the nineteenth century represented perhaps the high-water mark of the Chutes' management at the Prince's. After the death from tuberculosis of George Macready Chute in August 1888, his brother James, originally trained as an engineer, took sole control, and like every other manager he found the Bristol public 'a peculiar lot to cater for'. When Mrs Kendal, who as 'bright Madge Robertson, who can't be matched' had been the darling of Theatre Royal audiences in the early 'sixties, brought her company in November 1887 she was rapturously received and publicly piqued herself on how cordially she was remembered. In March 1897 it was a different story, and she told a *Bristol Evening News* reporter: 'I cannot aspire to the honour that some people claim, viz.: That I am a native of Bristol, and I am glad for my own sake that I am not. If I had been born in Bristol I should have thought Bristolians were very slow to support their own people.' Beerbohm Tree's first visit in November 1892 was so poorly supported that he promptly crossed Bristol off his list, and only with difficulty was he persuaded to try again five years later, when with *Trilby* he drew more rewarding houses.

Even the pantomimes, as tastefully lavish as they were money-spinning, could run into trouble. The last night of *The Babes in the Wood* on 18 February 1888 was spoiled by the antics of a small group in the gallery, who shouted down the manager, threw squibs on the stage during the ballet, and shot peas at the actresses. Though the disgruntled tried to blame students, it was proved that the group comprised 'one solicitor, one traveller, and three medical and two law students, the remainder being leading members of three local football clubs'.

Against these few unpleasantnesses must be set the many successes, from the repeated visits of the D'Oyly Carte to the popularisation of Wagner by the Carl Rosa Opera Company, and stars as contrasted as Little Tich and Henry Irving, whose Brodribb relatives still lived in the city, and who chose the Prince's for the premiere of Conan Doyle's *Story of Waterloo* on 21 September 1894. Every leading actor-manager and every new play of importance, as well as innumerable evanescent melodramas and musical comedies, came to the Prince's. It had a virtual monopoly of serious drama and large-scale musicals and grand opera, though Ben Greet made valiant attempts to introduce outdoor Shakespeare at the Bristol Zoo, his leading lady in 1890 being a youthful Mrs Patrick Campbell, who had then been on the stage for only two years.

No manager could have been more secure in the affections of the profession and the public than 'Jimmie' Chute. His success enabled him to have the theatre redecorated inside and out by Frank Matcham in 1889, and to introduce electricity in 1895. He certainly had no reason to worry about the Theatre Royal, but even the Prince's could be affected by the popularity of the big circus troupes which occupied the Drill Hall for at least two months of every year, and, during their brief visits, by Buffalo Bill Cody's Wild West Show or Barnum and Bailey's combination of circus, menagerie and fairground, 'The Greatest Show on Earth'.

Buffalo Bill's visit in September 1891 followed after one of Irving's engagements at the Prince's, and in a pleasant gesture of respect from one leading entertainer to another, Cody came over to Bristol a day early with some of his Indians to see Irving off at Temple Meads Station; 'they all shook hands and wished each other good luck.' Later that day the mile-long procession of animals, performers and their caravans made its way from the station to the show site off Gloucester Road, Bishopston, where seats for 15,000 spectators were erected. Barnum and Bailey, arriving in August 1898, brought traffic to a standstill as they went through the city to Bedminster, where three rings and two raised stages offered entertainment for 11,000 people; the following year when they set up in Bishop Road, Bishopston, the authorities insisted on an early-morning start for the procession, to avoid the appalling traffic jams previously created. It is noticeable that these shows, and the very few other tenting circuses, had now to seek sites in the outskirts, as the central areas of Bristol became fully built up.

Another important competitor to theatre arose in the opening years of the 'nineties: the 'family' variety house. Boxing Night 1892 saw the opening of Livermore's People's Palace in Baldwin Street, the shell of which now houses the Gaumont Cinema. The Livermore Brothers had for many years run a most successful costume concert party known as Livermore's Court Minstrels, which had played at the Colston Hall with considerable success, and with an eye to the future they also invested in what they were shrewd enough to see was the way organised entertainment was going. Their Bristol house, which seated 3,000, was part of a circuit—a new and ominous departure; 'conducted on temperance lines' and with considerable resources in the selection of artists, it soon won high tributes to its respectability and artistic standards from the Bristol press, and flourished well into the new century.

On 6 November the following year, Moss and Thornton opened the Empire Theatre of Varieties in Old Market Street. A preliminary announcement claimed:

It is admitted by all, except those who are blinded by their own prejudice and bigotry, that the people must have amusement, therefore the Directors consider that, in their endeavour to purify and raise the tone of the Music Hall entertainment, they are entitled to the good wishes and support of all right-minded persons. (Advertisement in *Bristol Times & Mirror*, 21.10.1893)

The Empire, like the People's Palace, was officially 'dry', but since the entrance was through the White Hart Inn this placed little restriction on thirsty members of the audience, a fact which increased their naturally rather boisterous manners, and militated against the Directors' good intentions.

There was trouble on the very first night, the theatre managers threatening a lawsuit if Cora Stuart appeared in a spoken sketch when the Empire possessed only a 'music and dancing' licence, so the sketch was altered to one involving singing only, a subterfuge with a long pedigree. Luxuriously fitted, lit by electricity (a novelty not then adopted by any 'legitimate' theatre in Bristol), and equipped with excellent stage facilities, the Empire could seat over 2,000 spectators, and in view of this and the success of the People's Palace it is not surprising that the theatre managers should feel their rivals looming over their shoulders, and react accordingly.

The Royal was of course particularly vulnerable; Melville's successor, John Barker, held out for only a year, and in June 1894 the management passed to Ernest Carpenter. Carpenter vigorously tackled the problem of finding paying attractions by trying out most of the theatrical possibilities in turn, including a return during the summer to a Stock Company in a weekly repertory thoroughly nostalgic of the 'sixties and 'seventies, but the Royal was too small and old fashioned for the better touring companies and its most accessible audiences were in no position to pay for quality. Seat prices had to be reduced steadily and gradually the repertoire became confined to melodrama and pantomime; by the end of the century it was difficult to get the audiences to accept anything else.

Meanwhile, the Empire was undergoing a succession of crises brought about primarily by the fact that the hall had been built, like the Royal, behind a frontage of other buildings, and the site had to be negotiated as a whole. The crippling mortgage ruined one lessee after another: Moss and Thornton's management lasted six months and attempts to refloat the controlling company ended in tragicomic bankruptcy proceedings. Later E. Leon attempted simultaneously to manage the Empire, the Star (in 1894 renamed, yet again, the Tivoli), and nine dentistry businesses; the attempt, not surprisingly, was shortlived.

Adopting one proverbial way of dealing with rivals, Ernest Carpenter bought his way into the ownership of the Empire, and capitalised on the exceptional stage facilities by making a feature of grand fairy spectacles and melodramatic sketches such as *The Jaws of Death*, in which

the villainy of the 'heavy man' was so cruel that some of the 'gods' became quite excited, and several times tried to warn the hero and heroine of the plot against them. (*Bristol Evening News*, 18.4.1899)

He even transferred the Christmas pantomime from the Royal to the Empire, but came to grief the following spring in a premature attempt to introduce twice-nightly variety, and sold his interest in the music hall.

The appeal of the big new halls, attracting every well known name in variety from Marie Lloyd to Sandow the Strong Man, overwhelmed the little Star-Tivoli. Because it was the only hall with a drinking licence there was always some hopeful applicant for management; in 1899 there was an attempt to promote the Grand Tivoli Lounge as 'the only Professional meeting house where the Artistes of Both Theatres and Both Music Halls meet daily'. Some sensation was caused in January the following year when Lady Ada Mansell took the lease, but neither her title nor her skill as a serio-comic artiste availed, and the Tivoli virtually expired with the reign of Victoria.

But, creeping in with ever-increasing frequency, were the 'animated pictures', the great mechanical novelty of the decade. Jerky, flickering, restricted in size of image and length of reel, the new items and comic sketches were greeted enthusiastically by all kinds of audiences, and often praised for their educational value by the press. Charles Gascoigne, the manager of the People's Palace, was an ardent cine-photographer himself and his films of local events were a feature of Palace programmes. The Theatre Royal occasionally introduced short films to top up an evening's entertainment; the Prince's even substituted a series of interest films for the Harlequinade in their pantomime of 1896–97; but it was the music halls which did most to popularise the new entertainment. In addition film producers sponsored demonstrations at halls throughout the city; as a technical development, film was already being taken seriously.

It is clear, however, that the managements of 'live' houses, so far from scenting possible rivalry, welcomed the moving pictures as an attractive novelty. They were soon to learn that they had fostered a cuckoo in their nests.

FIVE

Crises of Confidence

For a few years it was still possible for theatre managers to ignore the competition of the moving pictures. True, they had clearly come to stay: the Bioscope became a stock item in the weekly bill of the Empire, and Horace Livermore instituted a matinee 'Palace Hour' of family-type films at the Palace. When the Poole Brothers presented their Christmas Myrioramas an elderly Bristol resident recalled 60 years afterwards how

To conclude, that new-fangled invention, the cinematograph, would be shown on a screen lowered from the lofty ceiling, and scratchy pictures giving the appearance of continuous rain fussily projected from a small asbestos covered booth in the middle of the hall. (*Bristol Evening Post*, 16.9.1967)

In 1910 Pringle opened three picture-palaces (the shell of one, the Scala in Zetland Road, still remains), and the King's and Queen's Halls, both in Old Market Street, also opened the same year for films.

Another established competitor, the circus, had almost dropped out of the running by this time. Though Buffalo Bill revisited the city in 1903 and Sanger in 1906, they were forced out to sites in the suburbs, of which the favourite was the Rovers' football ground at Eastville: more evidence of the growth of an audience for popular entertainment in east Bristol. It was exceptional when the Royal Italian Circus appeared on old equestrian territory in 1911, taking over the skating rink in Rupert Street between the Centre and the Horsefair, and running twice nightly performances for five weeks.

So far as dramatic entertainments went, the Prince's and the Theatre Royal had little competition, thanks largely to the tightening of licensing regulations. Companies of Pastoral Players, made up mainly of Bensonians, still occasionally visited the Zoological Gardens, where Harcourt Williams staged that rarity, *The Two Gentlemen of Verona*, in July 1902.

Occasionally the Victoria Rooms was used for dramatic performances or recitals: William Poel brought *Everyman* there in December 1902, his own performance as Adonai being almost the only one to attract adverse criticism. In March 1911 Laurence Housman defied the censor's ban on his play *Pains and Penalties*, dealing with George IV and Queen Caroline, by giving a reading under the auspices of the Women's Social and Political Union. Recitalists at the Victoria Rooms included Albert Chevalier and, on 30 October 1911, Ellen Terry, whose now capricious memory inspired mingled delight and embarrassment in the spectators.

Over and above the whole entertainment, lay Miss Terry's womanliness. It was stamped all over the entire programme. It commenced with a womanly, we won't say unpunctuality, but a slight disregard of time, in commencing; and it ended with a womanly confession that to-night she was going to give another phase of Shakespeare's Heroines, as last night. They were the Triumphant Woman at—'I can't remember.' It was a real Ellen Terryism, and the reward of its ingenuousness was an outburst of applause from a very full hall. (*Western Daily Press*, 30.10.1911)

The Victoria Rooms also found itself being used as a wet-weather refuge for the ill-fated Adeler and Sutton's Olympic Pierrots, who set up a summer show in the open skating rink behind the Rooms and found themselves consistently rained off. Three weeks of the 'summer' of 1902 sufficed for this improbable venture, which was never repeated.

None of these activities affected a No. 1 touring theatre like the Prince's under James Macready Chute. His prosperity allowed him to undertake another major remodelling and redecoration in 1902 to designs by Frank Matcham, and to make further improvements to ventilation in 1907. He presented all the popular dramatic and musical comedy hits of the decade, and actor-managers like Benson, Martin Harvey, Oscar Asche and Wilson Barrett. Occasionally he would risk something a little more *avant-garde*: Granville Barker appeared in Shaw's *Man and Superman* in September 1908 when there was intense debate in Bristol on women's rights and suffrage, and a visit from Christabel Pankhurst herself was in prospect.

The class split between the Prince's and the Royal's audiences was almost complete by now; at the latter, outside the pantomime season, the sensational was relieved only by the sentimental. Ernest Carpenter had defined his audience, and would not risk presenting them with a possibly unpopular challenge. Some material alterations, however, were forced upon him: the now derelict houses fronting the theatre were pulled down in 1902 and a new entrance and suite of theatre offices opened in January 1903, only to be dangerously damaged by subsidence less than four years later as the result of irresponsible overloading of an adjacent warehouse.

When the Royal Patent fell due for renewal in 1903 the Lord Chamberlain instigated a safety check, and the hair-raising document submitted by his surveyor involved the Proprietors in something like £1,150 expenditure additional to the £2,375 already laid out for the new frontage. Even then, not all the Lord Chamberlain's requirements could be met, but as the first stage of improvements satisfied the Bristol police, Carpenter made a virtue of necessity and without reference to the Proprietors obtained a local licence, making the Patent superfluous. He himself belatedly installed electric light in the autumn of 1905, but other internal structural improvements he desired, especially a fly-tower, were turned down by the financially-harassed Proprietors.

As a commercial manager pursuing a 'lowest common denominator' policy, Carpenter was highly competent and reasonably successful. The most dangerous rivalry came not from the Prince's but from the two big Bristol music halls, especially after Sid Macaire and Harry Day became successively associated with the Empire management and gradually won a more settled prosperity for that erratically-financed enterprise. Sketches played an increasingly important part in their programmes, a national 'gentlemen's agreement' restraining legal action by theatre proprietors. By March 1908 an actor of the stature of Laurence Irving could appear successfully at the Empire in a light comedy duologue, *The Dog Between*. Another sketch presented later that year at the Palace appealed perhaps to less elevated sensibilities: *A Society Woman*, 'Including the most Realistic and Sensational Fight between a Man and Woman ever seen on the Variety Stage. SEE THE SMASHING OF MIRRORS, FURNITURE, AND THE WRECKAGE OF A LUXURIOUS HOME.'

Then between 1909 and 1915 the whole balance of entertainment changed. Both theatres lost key figures: Ernest Carpenter died at Christmas 1909 and his widow, who inherited his interest in the lease, had no pretensions to management; the death of J. M. Chute on 15 February 1912 led to a limited liability company being formed to take over the running of the Prince's. There was a sudden expansion of music-hall entertainment, Walter de Frece opening his Bedminster Hippodrome south of the river on 7 August 1911 just as Oswald Stoll stepped on to the Bristol scene, dazzling the normally anti-theatre magistrates into promising him a licence for a new Hippodrome to be built in St Augustine's Parade.

Stoll's proposals, publicised in the *Western Daily Press* of 2 May 1911, caused consternation among existing managements. Within two months the Empire had applied (unsuccessfully) for a dramatic licence; the pretext that they wanted to legalise the sketches they had been putting on for nearly 20 years deceived nobody. Horace Livermore, who had now taken over personal control of the Palace, admitted at the hearing of Stoll's application that the success of the Empire had hit him hard, and a rich competitor operating within 100 yards of his premises was the last straw. He restructured his programme, returning to his old friends the Court Minstrels, whose performances were varied with the presentation of 'Living Speaking Pictures' in which local actors delivered dialogue in synchronisation with the screen picture. Almost imperceptibly the Palace became an acknowledged picture house, though for years yet it included some variety acts between the reels.

The new Bedminster Hippodrome never really established itself, despite some enterprising engagements such as a flying matinee of Adeline Genée in October 1911 and a visit of the Beecham Opera Company in June 1912. Repeatedly de Frece tried to obtain an alternative drama licence; repeatedly he was blocked by the opposition of the theatre managers, reluctant to admit that any new audience could be won without affecting their already marginal profits. Finally in 1914 de Frece gave up and sold out to Stoll, who reopened the building as a cinema in April 1915, leaving the south of Bristol once more without live entertainment.

Nothing, indeed, could compete with the richly-decorated, splendidly-equipped Hippodrome with its vast stage and huge tanks for water spectacles. Its programmes, backed by the resources of the Stoll organisation, brought not only music hall personalities like Little Tich, George Formby, W. C. Fields and Albert Chevalier, but stage stars in serious one-act plays and even scenes from Shakespeare. It was in fact possible to see more leading theatrical figures on the halls than in the theatre proper, and when Sarah Bernhardt and her company gave a half-hour selection from *La Dame aux Camélias* in October 1913 to a packed and hushed audience, it must have been clear that music hall had acquired a completely new image, and that the theatre would do well to adapt accordingly.

Frederick Carpenter, running the Royal on his sister-in-law's behalf, realised this, and with the moral support of the Bristol Playgoers' Club, attempted to capitalise on the rising repertory movement. In December 1913 he engaged for two weeks Miss Horniman's Gaiety Theatre Company, including Lewis Casson and Sybil Thorndike, and in May 1914 he let his theatre for an experimental season to Muriel Pratt, a breakaway member of the same company. Sadly, the outbreak of World War I, the enforced Christmas break (when unsympathetic magistrates refused Miss Pratt permission to use an alternative hall during the inevitable pantomime), and in May 1915 the Carpenters' bankruptcy dealt fatal blows to an under-capitalised enterprise. In the hands of a dubious syndicate, Bristol Theatres Ltd, and its even more dubious nominee, Cecil Hamilton Baines, who somehow persuaded Mrs Carpenter's trustee in bankruptcy to let them take over the lease, the Royal reverted to a cheaper version of Ernest Carpenter's policy of melodrama and pantomime, while the building was allowed to deteriorate into a slum.

Though it is only too probable that Fred Carpenter's attempt to vary his theatre's fare arose from desperation rather than idealism, at last he showed more flexibility in the face of the cut-throat opposition of the music halls and cinemas than did the Prince's under the board of management set up after J. M. Chute's death. Neither building nor clientèle encouraged change, so it continued as a touring house with gradually lessening support: in 1915 the summer vacation was extended to eight weeks. More and more the new management relied on light entertainment to relieve the stresses of war and its aftermath; by 1919, apart from a fortnight's visit of the Carl Rosa Opera Company (which included the premiere of Somerville's *The Miracle*) and appearances by Martin Harvey and Fred Terry, there were only two weeks of drama against eleven of pantomime, 18 of musicals and ten of comedies.

Small wonder that the call for a repertory theatre with worthwhile plays became more and more insistent. In 1923 the Rotary Club, led by its President J. E. Barton (headmaster of Bristol Grammar School) and Secretary A. E. Stanley Hill, leased from the Corporation the Lesser Colston Hall, renamed it the Little Theatre and appointed as producer Rupert Harvey, an experienced member of the Old Vic Company. The Hall was a 'shoe-box' cube with a stage possessing just three feet of wing space, only an underground passage from OP to PS for performers and an incredibly inconvenient and cramped 'get-out' for scenery and props, but ingenuity and enthusiasm triumphed over the disadvantages. The venture was launched on 17 December 1923 by Sir Arthur Pinero with a short speech which seemed interminable to the actor waiting to speak the first words of the play: Ralph Hutton, stalwart of the Little Theatre till his fatal collapse in the wings 20 years later.

Other changes were taking place in the postwar pattern of entertainment. Old-style music hall was yielding to variety and revue, and Harry Day, now an MP but still energetically running the Empire, was using that theatre increasingly for the premieres of many of his London-bound revues. In 1922 he at last succeeded in procuring a stage licence, which enable him to vary his programmes with the occasional play, such as *A Roof and Four Walls* with Phyllis Neilson-Terry. At the Hippodrome, managed by the popular S. Fortescue Harrison, there was a remarkable range of attractions within its variety and revue programmes: in 1923 alone they included Beatrice Lillie, Will Fyffe, Gracie Fields in *Mr Tower of London* (previously staged at the Empire), Shaw's *The Showing Up of Blanco Posnet*, and Hengler's Circus.

Shortly after the war the Victoria Rooms was bought by Sir George Wills and presented to the University Union, and this left no properly equipped hall suitable for recitals or small-scale touring productions outside the main stream. All Saints' Parish Hall in Clifton was used for performances of Greek plays in Gilbert Murray's translation in December 1921, and in 1923 a concert pavilion was built in an abandoned quarry at the top of Blackboy Hill on the Downs, known as The Glen; this was occupied during several summers by 'refined pierrot entertainments' and military bands. The alternative to such makeshift premises was the large Colston Hall, which was adapted for a number of shows for which it was by no means architecturally suitable. One such was a financially disastrous visit in May 1921 by the Glastonbury Players under Rutland Boughton, with Gwen Ffrancon-Davies and Frederick Woodhouse in *The Immortal Hour*; by contrast a ballet performance by Pavlova and her company two months later packed the hall for a matinee and evening performance.

Compared with the previous decade, there was something of a revival of the drama in the early 'twenties, as the establishment of the Little Theatre attested. The Prince's repertoire became more balanced and even Shakespeare once again attracted the crowds with the arrival in 1920 of the young Henry Baynton, whose energy and personal magnetism brought standing ovations from audiences for whom the glories of Benson had become somewhat faded. Its predominantly middle-class

48

audience enabled the Prince's to ride out the effects of the labour troubles of the mid-twenties which culminated in the General Strike of 1926.

The Royal was less fortunately situated. Under Hamilton Baines the theatre sank to its lowest level yet, and by the time Baines and Bristol Theatres Ltd had gone bankrupt in rapid and unsurprising succession in 1923–4, the building was so nearly derelict and in such social disrepute that even those most conscious of its old glories thought its closure must be final. The principal effect indeed seemed to fall less on the public than on the public houses, the licensee of *The Naval Volunteer* in King Street blaming her financial failure on 'bad trade through the closing of the Theatre Royal'.

Finally in 1924 the premises were leased, and in the following year bought, by a consortium of three managers, Robert Courtneidge, Milton Bode and Douglas Millar, the last-named being the active partner and licensee. No greater contrast to Baines could be imagined: ignoring the crippling rheumatism from which he suffered, Millar tackled the rehabilitation of the Royal with enthusiasm, cleaning, rewiring and redecorating the sadly dilapidated premises before opening at Christmas 1924 with a highly successful pantomime, *Aladdin*, which ran until 21 March.

Then came the crucial difficulty: what to do for the main part of the season? Undoubtedly Millar had many well-wishers in his attempt to restore the glories of the Royal, but most of them still had an inbuilt disinclination to penetrate the down-at-heel dock area of King Street. To combat this, Millar made serious attempts to link up with the better amateur societies, to encourage local playwrights, and generally to integrate his theatre with the city's life. But the faithful Royal theatre-goers were still the unsophisticated followers of melodrama, and despite individual successes Millar found his audience compelled him to compromise in his policy. The General Strike wrecked one of his most ambitious efforts, Basil Hood's *Young England*, cast from the cream of Bristol amateurs, and after this failure Millar reverted to the old ways, every attempt to move in a higher direction being thwarted by the insistent laws of profit and loss. A deeply disappointed man, he sold out his share in the Theatre Royal in 1931 and retired.

One reason, of course, that Millar found it so difficult to gain the audience for serious drama he hoped for, lay in the artistic success of the Little Theatre under Rupert Harvey and, after his resignation through ill-health in 1926, Alfred Brooks and Ralph Hutton. They maintained a good quality company, giving opportunities to players of the calibre of Sebastian Shaw and Marjorie Fielding, and to several actors who later made their names in other theatrical careers, such as Laurier Lister and the playwrights Arthur Macrae and Philip King. The last-named particularly was very highly regarded as an all-round actor, and when he left the company in June 1932 after four years, the *Western Daily Press* wrote:

Few repertory companies can claim such a fine representative of their task, their triumphs, and their ideals as Philip King.

Financially, the results were less happy: as the decade wore on, live entertainment met increasing competition from the 'talkies', and after six seasons the Rotary Club had had enough of meeting the Little Theatre deficits. As a programme note put it, 'The Rotary Club may be benefactors, but they cannot afford to be philanthropists.' Instead, a private company, Bristol's Little Theatre Ltd, was formed in 1929; Stanley Hill became its managing director and used profits from his annual Bristol Ideal Homes Exhibition to subsidise the Little. The production policy remained essentially unchanged: a lively mixture of good commercial theatre, late Victorian and Edwardian revivals, at least one new play a season, often by a local author, and such classics as the cramped stage permitted. Barrie and Shaw were favourite authors: *Back to Methuselah* was staged in its entirety in 1929.

It is arguable that there was by now an overprovision of drama in Bristol, as happened again in 1973, especially in view of the worsening economic situation. When the Regent Cinema, Castle Street (on the site of an illicit boxing booth of the 'nineties) applied for a stage licence in 1928, the theatres joined in opposition, Douglas Millar admitting that he had lost £2,000 when he booked touring companies which could not get dates at the Prince's; 'he could not exist without the annual pantomime'. The Regent's application was, predictably, refused, but even so the competition provided by the cinemas was increasing in quantity, variety and quality. By 1928 there were over 30 cinemas in Bristol, and a number of these also had 'singing and dancing' licences which enabled them to insert individual 'turns' between features. (At the King's, in Old Market Street, in 1926, one of these was billed as 'Natcha Rompa, The Famous Oriental Dancer'—a name worthy of ITMA.)

The music halls, already uncertain of their artistic development, felt the impact even more. In April 1931 the Empire was taken over by ABC as 'Bristol's Popular Super-Talkie Cinema' and in October 1932 even the Bristol Hippodrome succumbed. Bristol was left without a variety theatre, though this did not mean the total disappearance of this form of entertainment. Local impresario Charles Lockyer occasionally hired the Colston Hall for variety programmes, for which the new accent on 'big bands' now made it more suitable, and even the Drill Hall in Old Market Street was occasionally pressed into service. The new manager at the Theatre Royal, William King, quickly switched from melodrama to girlie shows, advertised, significantly, as 'Super Revues at Cinema Prices', and scored a considerable popular success with them. An *Evening World* correspondent in March 1932 wrote of his pleasure at being able to obtain a Dress Circle seat for only 1s 3d (6p) including Early Doors charge:

Now that is what I call a reasonable price for working people, and the show [*Hot Nights*] was simply splendid.

Even the Prince's saw a much-needed opportunity to profit from the situation. In 1935 the management sought and obtained a licence to put on variety shows in the summer at reduced prices. During the previous three seasons they had lost, successively, £1,286, £678 and £862, said Mr F. G. Tricks, Chairman of the Company, and

they felt that the dramatic season must be subsidised some way or the other, otherwise it would mean they would have to open the theatre for dramatic purposes practically six weeks in the spring, then close it and open again in October, November and December.

Another factor was the increasing reluctance of London stars to tour the provinces. 'We get the best we can. Sometimes we get a week we do not know how to fill in,' Tricks admitted. (*Bristol Evening Post*, 4.3.1935)

The Little, ever precariously balanced financially, was hit especially hard by the depression of the 'thirties. In June 1934, because of inadequate public support, Bristol's Little Theatre Ltd put on its last production: with typical spirit, this was a brand-new play about the Tolpuddle Martyrs, *Mortal Fingers* by Martha Scott. It was particularly ironic that the company should have been forced to disband within two months of winning the *Sunday Referee* plaque for its 'exceptional artistic standards'.

Alfred Brooks, one of the producers, tried a five-week season in July and August; in September Gerard Neville and Kathleen Barbour, who had been running repertory at Bath, took over, but their unenterprising programme was a sad drop in standards and at the beginning of 1935 they in turn were succeeded by Ronald Russell, an Old Cliftonian who had joined the Little as a student in 1929. He was backed financially by Grizel Kinross, and with Stanley Hill as a sort of lingering *éminence grise* they formed The Rapier Players Ltd, their original ten weeks season being extended to 22.

But the way was very far from clear. Hill was prone to dabble in questions of casting (astonishingly, he complained that Peggy Ann Wood lacked charm); he quarrelled with both Russell and Grizel Kinross and finally resigned in April 1936, in the midst of another financial crisis, which was only overcome when a supporter offered £50 towards the current appeal for a Reserve Fund provided five others would do likewise—which happily they did. By the beginning of June the Fund had reached £855. The following year three of the Little's most popular actors were recruited: Michael Hordern, Lockwood West and Paul Lorraine; and regular support began to increase encouragingly.

In the end, the film industry overreached itself. By 1938 there were simply not enough features of reasonable standard to fill the cinemas, yet new picture-houses were still going up. Early that year Sir Oswald Stoll announced that the Hippodrome would revert to variety, alternating with ice spectacles, from 1 August, and the following year the Empire followed suit.

Other branches of entertainment reflected the same new liveliness; circuses became irregular visitors again, usually at the Drill Hall, and the Victoria Rooms (gutted by fire in 1934 but rebuilt with vastly improved stage facilities) became available not only for good-class amateur shows but for professional dance companies like the Ballets

Jooss, who paid their first visit to Bristol in April 1938, and in 1940 the Ballet Trois Arts and the Lydia Kyasht Ballet.

The second World War had a much greater impact on live entertainment, both direct and indirect, than the first. Initially the black-out and the curtailment of public transport had a depressing effect on attendances, leading the Empire into yet another bankruptcy. Interruptions to train services led to many difficulties. On one Monday in January 1940 the Empire orchestra found itself giving a veritable concert till the delayed company could get to the theatre; the Prince's, for the first time in over ten years, was forced to put in an understudy for a principal artist; and Tommy Handley, at the Hippodrome, had to 'borrow' Jack Train to take over a minor part in his Disorderly Room sketch in the absence of the missing bit-player.

With the air raids came disaster. In the very first blitz, that of the night of 24 November 1940, the Prince's was completely demolished, and several cinemas capable of staging live shows, including the Regent, the Bedminster Hippodrome and the Triangle, were also destroyed by enemy action. The Hippodrome, *faute de mieux*, became now a touring theatre for plays, ballet and opera as well as summer variety, though the building was not entirely suitable either behind or before the curtain, the pit bar being actually in the auditorium, and the acoustics placing a strain on even experienced professional actors.

Though not itself badly damaged, conditions in the area forced the Empire to close from November 1940 to the following February, and the Little Theatre found a 'matinees only' programme so crippling financially that the Rapier Players went on tour in mid-December and did not return until Easter Saturday 1941—when the aftermath of yet another raid left them without electricity until little more than an hour before the curtain was due to rise.

Amazingly the Royal was scarcely touched by bombing, but it was suffering sufficiently from other causes. Milton Bode died in 1938, Courtneidge in 1939, and though King kept the theatre running after a fashion it was again in appalling condition, performers being liable to find they had put a foot right through the stage; after the blitz of 16–17 March 1941 the Royal was closed, to all appearances permanently, and put up for auction early in 1942. Through the energy and idealism of members of the Council for the Preservation of Ancient Bristol, and the unselfish co-operation of Mr C. H. W. Davey of the Metal Agencies Company, who had intended buying the building as a warehouse, the theatre was bought at auction for £10,500, and an appeal was launched to cover the purchase money and the cost of essential repairs. The upshot was crisply summarised in an *Evening World* editorial of 29 January 1943:

Bristol was asked to provide enough money to buy the Theatre Royal. Bristol put its hand in its pocket, took out a handful of coins, put back the silver, and handed over the coppers. So of the £20,000 wanted only £4,672 has been contributed.

Members of the Preservation Fund Committee guaranteed a bank loan to cover the balance.

Licences to carry out the vital repair work caused more difficulties, and these had not been solved when the wartime Council for the Encouragement of Music and the Arts offered to lease the theatre, put it in order and maintain it, paying the bank-loan interest as part of the rental, and ploughing back any profits to repay the guarantors (which it was able to do within six years). It was not an enviable assignment: as Charles Landstone, the Deputy Drama Director of CEMA, reported shortly before the reopening on 11 May 1943,

As soon as decorating or restoration is attempted the rotting 170-year-old timbers give way, and it is necessary to put in new steel trusses. . . The estimate given at the last [Drama] Panel meeting was £6,300, up to the opening date. It will today be safer to say £7,500.

Despite unavoidable restrictions, excellent work was done in restoring the original green-and-gold colour scheme, raking the pit and providing stalls seats, and reseating the gallery with padded benches instead of wooden ones.

The work of CEMA and ENSA in promoting touring companies of high quality during the war ensured a supply of interesting new plays and classical revivals for the Royal, which benefited, as did every other Bristol theatre, by the tremendous wartime boom in entertainment. The end of the war, however, brought both disasters and challenges. In February 1945, the main Colston Hall, which had gone almost unscathed through the war despite its central position, burned down; weekday concerts were transferred to the Methodist Central Hall in Old Market Street and Sunday engagements to the Embassy Cinema near the Victoria Rooms. It was six years before the Colston Hall could be rebuilt, and when it was, though its concert acoustics continued to be first class, those for speech were so patchy that after one or two attempts any idea of dramatic shows without amplifiers had to be given up. In 1947 the Prince's Theatre owners finally realised that they had no hope of raising the money necessary to rebuild, and sold out to the Stoll Theatre Corporation, owners of the Hippodrome.

The Empire once again ran into difficulties. During the war the management had eked out the staple fare of revue with a wide range of entertainments, from the Polish Ballet to Brieux's *Damaged Goods*, and from pantomime to the Royal Imperial Circus. The latter started its engagement a day late, as owing to the aberrations of a zoologically-confused railwayman at Bournemouth the preceding weekend, the circus troupe unloaded props and scenery for Lillian Hellman's play *The Little Foxes*, while at the Norwich theatre an equally surprised manager 'found himself landed with performing dogs, monkeys and ponies, plus the complete company of "Little Foxes".' (*Bristol Evening World*, 30.8.1943.) After the war troubles increased. Lurid dramas (one was advertised as 'The play that shocked the *News of the World*') or more respectable repertory offered by Harry Hanson's Court Players were equally unsuccessful; eventually the Empire went back to almost uninterrupted revue of the kind which had kept the Theatre Royal afloat in prewar days, and which doubtless drew on the same, now displaced, audience.

Officially sponsored tours closed down after the war even more quickly than the commercial ones, and the smallness of the Royal and its restricted stage facilities once more militated against its success. This problem was triumphantly solved when the Arts Council of Great Britain (as CEMA became in peacetime) invited the Old Vic to organise a Company at the Theatre Royal. Under Hugh Hunt's sometimes extravagant, occasionally idiosyncratic, but always positive direction, the Bristol Old Vic quickly established itself, and a three-weekly repertory proved practicable in only the second season.

Then on 16 February 1948 a serious fire at the Hippodrome almost completely destroyed the stage and dressing rooms, taking out of action yet another of Bristol's major halls. The *Evening Post* estimated that a pre-war seating capacity of 13,000 had now been halved. Intensive pressure by the Corporation as well as by Stoll Theatres secured a repair licence, but the Hippodrome was shut for the rest of the year.

The results of the fire were far-reaching. The Empire, just about to seek a licence to convert to a dance hall, decided to postpone this action, and even took over one or two Hippodrome bookings. All theatre fire precautions were checked: the Little was closed for three months in the summer of 1948, and the Royal shut in June 1949 for alterations—many of them just those for which the Lord Chamberlain had been pressing back in 1902 and which Carpenter had then sidestepped. This time work was suddenly stopped after only two months because of unexpected extra costs; in a premature panic all staff, including Hugh Hunt's successor as Bristol Old Vic Director, Allan Davis, were given notice. The resulting uproar not only pressured the Arts Council into providing the additional money, but moved Bristol Corporation to take a direct interest in the running and financing of the Theatre Royal.

The six-month closure presented the Rapier Players at the Little with an opportunity once again to be more adventurous in their choice of plays; the competition of the Old Vic, with its 'quality' repertory, and the financial pressures of trying to change from a weekly to a fortnightly system, had meant an increasingly conventional programme. With the Theatre Royal shut they were less restricted—there was, for example, an outstanding production of Tennessee Williams' *Glass Menagerie*—and they were at length able to establish fortnightly repertory on a permanent basis.

Another effect of the Bristol Old Vic's presence had been to encourage the development of the University Drama Department; founded in 1947, it was the first of its kind in Great Britain. Initially as one element in a General Arts degree, then as part of a Joint Honours BA, and ultimately as a degree subject in its own right, theatre became an increasingly accepted academic study. In 1951 a squash court in the Wills Building was cleverly adapted by Richard Southern to serve as an experimental theatre, and it was here that the premiere of Pinter's *The Room* took place in 1957. A grant from the Rockefeller Foundation in 1956 financed a Fellowship in Playwriting, whose holders included John Arden; Arden's *The Happy Haven* had its first performance in the Studio Theatre in 1960.[1]

While the study of theatre flourished, however, commercial entertainment was once more on the wane, this time owing mainly to the competition of television; one after another cinemas closed and by 1954 Bristol theatres were facing a major slump. The Empire, threatened additionally with eventual demolition for road improvements, closed in August 1954; it was bought by the City Council and leased to the BBC as a studio for the last nine years of its life. Stoll Theatres sold off part of the intended New Prince's site, and it became obvious that the Park Row theatre would never be rebuilt, especially as the Hippodrome was in difficulties. The virtual collapse of touring made it hard to keep the theatre continuously open, especially after variety finally petered out and left the summer weeks vacant. As for the Little, box-office receipts for the 1953-4 season were the lowest for six years. Even the Royal temporarily lost impetus following the departure after four seasons of Director Denis Carey, whose crusading enthusiasm won him an unrivalled place in the affections of Bristolians and made it difficult for succeeding Directors with less personality to establish themselves.

Over the next seven years financial difficulties increased, especially after 1957, when commercial television came to the southwest. 1961 brought a major crisis to the Rapier Players who in January gave warning that without subsidy they could continue for no more than another 18 months; the Arts Council, however, rejected a plea for help mainly because it 'was already substantially aiding one theatre in a town which was fortunate enough to have three theatres, whilst there were in England many towns with one or no theatre.' The Corporation debated—and postponed action, for they were already deeply involved in discussions about the future of the Theatre Royal after the Arts Council's lease ran out in 1963. The prestige of the Bristol Old Vic won; in July 1962 the Corporation agreed to take over the lease of the Royal, and when Ronald Russell finally gave notice in November 1962, the Bristol Old Vic were offered the Little Theatre also, enabling them to run an interchangeable double company.

Neither memories of Lewis Casson's 1943 assurance that he would 'hate to think that anything we did at the Theatre Royal was likely to damage [the Rapier Players]' nor a belated announcement by the Drama Director of the Arts Council that 'if Mr Russell cared to apply for a grant in respect of the 1963–64 financial year it would be sympathetically considered' can have much comforted Ronald Russell for this shabby ending to his 28 years' service to the city's entertainment.

Considerable improvements to stage and auditorium of the Little were carried out in 1964, but the Bristol Old Vic did not seem able to exploit their new acquisition. Audiences do not change their tastes

---

[1] In 1961, on the expiry of the grant, Television Wales and the West endowed a Fellowship in Drama in memory of Lord Cilcennin.

quickly; theatres take time to establish new reputations. Attempts by Val May, who became Artistic Director of the Bristol Old Vic in 1961, to use the smaller theatre for relatively *avant-garde* productions such as a season of plays by Bristolian Charles Wood, came sadly to grief, and for some time the repertory was a slightly watered-down variant of that of the Royal, incorporating a proportion of West End thrillers and farces as a sop to the former Rapier Players patrons. Such productions as Pinter's *Homecoming* in 1967 aroused sharp protests, but gradually a younger and broader-minded audience was built-up.

The Hippodrome went from crisis to crisis. Though by now the only theatre in southwest England capable of housing big shows, there were relatively few of these on the road, and profit or loss was equally unpredictable. In 1967 alone the Hippodrome lost £4,000 on the musical *Robert and Elizabeth*, and £5,000 on the Rumanian National Dance Company. Even the Royal Shakespeare Company with Dorothy Tutin in *As You Like It* and Peggy Ashcroft in *Ghosts* (only its second production in Bristol) were greeted with sparse houses, and except for a week of Spike Milligan in *The Bed-Sitting Room* the theatre had to close from the end of June to mid-September.

There were however signs of revival in other forms of live entertainment. In 1964 William and Jean Poeton founded the Bristol Arts Centre in King Square, and the intimate theatre there encouraged the staging, mainly though not exclusively by amateurs, of both new plays and rare revivals. In 1967, for example, Max Adrian gave his one-man show, *Max Adrian as GBS*, and Charles Wood's *Dingo* was premiered shortly afterwards. In pubs and clubs live entertainment flourished again: folk singers, pop groups, cabaret artists, strippers; even that magnificent Victorian piece of Bristol Byzantine architecture, The Granary on Welsh Back, was leased by Acker Bilk in 1967 as a licensed jazz club.

Bristol University Drama Department moved to new premises in Park Row almost opposite the Prince's site, and acquired a new adaptable theatre, the Vandyck, used chiefly by the University and by the Bristol Old Vic Theatre School, but occasionally also by visiting professional companies. Mecca built an Entertainment Centre in Frogmore Street at the back of the Hippodrome, and took over The Glen, running it as a Dance and Olde Tyme Music Hall—that almost totally phoney piece of nostalgia which suddenly sprang into national popularity at this time.

The Theatre Royal reached a new peak of success, celebrating its 200th anniversary in 1966 with a notable season. Plans were laid for the rehabilitation of the next-door Coopers' Hall (which for many years had been a fruit warehouse) to provide a new and more imposing entrance; for the demolition of the 1902 offices fronting King Street and their replacement with a small experimental theatre; and for improving backstage facilities at the Royal itself, which were not only extremely cramped but were suffering from subsidence of the now heavily developed marshland between King Street and Baldwin Street.

That the last part of this scheme, necessary as it was, involved demolition of a large part of a building designated as a Historical Monument, was understandably not mentioned in the Appeal brochures; representations to the Minstry of Public Buildings and Works were met, long after elaborate publicity had taken place, with bland assurances that no official plans had been submitted. When at length he was forced to admit the existence of such plans, the Minister claimed, quite incorrectly, that 'the only part of the theatre which is actually scheduled as an ancient monument is the auditorium', and hinted that objections to the replanning project might 'lead to the abandonment of the modernisation proposals. In that case some other use would have to be found for the theatre and the whole structure might be put in jeopardy.' (Letter of 4 January 1970 from Mr John Silkin to the Council for the Preservation of Ancient Bristol). Thus it proved impossible to put forward for consideration alternative architect-backed suggestions which would have limited destruction of unique historic features while permitting essential stage, scenic and dressing-room improvements.

The Royal closed on 2 May 1970; by the winter demolition had left the auditorium, blocked up by corrugated iron sheets, isolated like a shabby tin hut in a sea of mud, and once freed of supporting accretions the structural weaknesses of a 200-year-old building erected on marshland became ever more apparent. Consequent additional costs, inflation and a public spending crisis played havoc with estimates and with response to the Appeal, and only a loan of £150,000 from the Bristol & West Building Society permitted sufficient work to be completed for the reopening in January 1972 of the exquisitely restored Coopers' Hall (to which the civic grant was largely devoted) and a serviceable but in many respects unfinished Theatre Royal. The experimental New Vic was built with the help of a Gulbenkian Foundation grant and opened five months later.

During the 20 months the Theatre Royal was closed, the Bristol Old Vic was virtually confined to the Little Theatre,[1] and the restrictions of the small house coupled with an uneven standard of production diminished support for the Bristol Old Vic as a whole. The Royal reopened on 12 January 1972 with a highly successful musical, *Trelawny*, but attendance after the first two productions fell to a little over 50 per cent. and the Little Theatre was no better supported. The reasons adduced were various, from unpopular choice of plays to uncomfortable seating; there was also growing disenchantment with Val May's interpretation of the role of Bristol Old Vic Director. It had become noticeable how selective he had latterly been in the plays he had himself directed, and how wary an eye he had kept on the potential West End transfer—almost every new play done at the Bristol Old Vic was in effect a preview for some West End management, as Ronald Hayman has pointed out.[2] There were good reasons for this, but it all tended to erode those all-important local roots, the sense of 'belonging' by which a provincial city sets such store.

[1] An experimental season at the Theatre Royal, Bath, came to grief, mainly because of a too-adventurous programme.
[2] In *The Set-Up: An Anatomy of the English Theatre Today* (Eyre Methuen, 1973, 124–5).

Whatever the cause, the drop in public confidence was only too apparent. A season based entirely on recent West End successes was tried in the spring of 1973; then in the autumn Peter O'Toole, Edward Hardwicke and Nigel Stock, all stars who had spent early seasons with the Bristol Old Vic, were persuaded to return for three productions and brought packed houses. Popularity returned to the Theatre Royal, but the wave of conservatism, approaching philistinism, among its audience combined with financial pressures to reduce the adventurousness of the repertoire far below the level of earlier years, and a promising programme of Theatre in Education built up by Mark Woolgar was jettisoned after he left.

As Douglas Morris, Bristol Old Vic General Manager, admitted, 'It was difficult to play to full houses simultaneously at all three theatres', and the role of the other parts of the Bristol Old Vic complex is still in debate. In 1973 poor support led to the curtailment of the Little Theatre season, and though it was the Golden Jubilee of repertory there were in the autumn only three productions, *Twelfth Night* (which had been produced in the Little's first season), *Blithe Spirit*, and Frisby's West End farce, *There's a Girl in My Soup*; the spring season consisted of three comedies and a thriller. The City Council at one point were clearly dubious about continuing the lease and even meditated turning the Little into a quality film cinema or a home for amateur drama, but finally continued the Old Vic tenancy, though with shorter seasons.

The New Vic, as the small studio theatre was called, scored heavily with some highly controversial documentaries, especially one on the Bristol Ring-Road Project, but some of its experimental work was very poorly supported; a quite sudden redirection towards 'safer' subjects brought the resignation of Associate Director Howard Davies and was partly, at least, responsible for the setting up of the Avon Touring Company in April 1974. Indeed it is to this Company, to various attempts at setting up Street Theatres, add to the challenging, if baffling, Crystal Theatre of the Saint (now, alas, based in Holland) that experiment and the search for the lost 'popular' audience for entertainment have largely passed.

It remains to be seen whether, with a change of Director in the autumn of 1975, the Bristol Old Vic will be able to regain artistic initiative and rebuild an audience prepared to support this, despite the impact of spiralling costs and the imperilling of public grants. The Arts Council's establishment of a special department to co-ordinate touring (DALTA) has brought some assistance to the Hippodrome, but with even the big national companies cutting back on provincial visits, its future outside the pantomime season must still be regarded as unsettled.

But the lesson of the past is that live entertainment, though it may change in form and accent, meets a need too deep-seated ever to disappear: as Professor Arthur Skemp put it 60 years ago, there is no art 'so vivid, so various, so potent in its address to the imagniation, as that art which makes imagined life move and have its being before our eyes'. (Letter in *Western Daily Press*, 23.6.1914).

Principal Sources

CENTRAL LIBRARY, BRISTOL

Bristol newspapers from 1726 onwards

Richard Smith Collection (five volumes of playbills, cuttings &c. relating to Bristol theatres up to 1835)

Account Book for Jacob's Wells Theatre, 1741–48

Complete set of playbills and programmes for New Theatre Royal/Prince's Theatre; programmes and cuttings for other Bristol theatres and music halls

BRISTOL ARCHIVES OFFICE

Legal documents, playbills &c. relating to Theatre Royal

Working papers for MA thesis (University of Bristol, 1935) by Rev N. F. Hulbert: A Historical Survey of the Somerset and Bristol Fairs

Programmes, photographs and Minute Books of Rapier Players

SOCIETY OF MERCHANT VENTURERS' ARCHIVES

Documents and Minutes relating to Jacob's Wells Theatre and 82 Castle Street

BOOKS

Richard Jenkins: *Memoirs of the Bristol Stage*, 1826

J. Tucker Murray: *English Dramatic Companies 1558–1642*, 2 vols, 1910

G. Tracey Watts: *Theatrical Bristol*, 1915

G. Rennie Powell: *The Bristol Stage—Its Story*, 1919

Rapier Players: *The Little Theatre, Bristol*, 1948

John Latimer: *The Annals of Bristol*, reprinted in 3 vols, 1970

Kathleen Barker: *The Theatre Royal, Bristol, 1766–1966*, 1974

PAMPHLET

Kathleen Barker: *Entertainment in the Nineties*, Bristol Branch of the Historical Association, 1973

ARTICLES

F. G. Lewin *et al.*: Bristol Amusement Houses of the Past. *Bristol Times & Mirror*, 26.1, 14.4, 12 & 19.5.1923

Kathleen Barker: The Assembly Rooms, *Bristol Evening Post*, 5.9.1956.

J. R. T. Coe: Bristol Hippodrome. *Evening Post*, 4, 5, 6, 7 & 8.12.1972; letters from readers 23.12.1972

New Theatre Magazine, X (issue on Street Theatre)

Kathleen Barker: An Early Seventeenth Century Provincial Playhouse. *Theatre Notebook*, XXIX, 2, 81–4

Index

63